Robert Francis Kennedy

Biography

of a

Compulsive Politician

by

Allen Roberts

Library of Congress Cataloging in Publication Data

Roberts, Allen.
  Robert Francis Kennedy: biography of a compulsive
politician.

    1. Kennedy, Robert F., 1925-1968. 2. United States—
Politics and government—1963-1969. 3. Legislators—
United States—Biography. 4. United States. Congress.
Senate—Biography. I. Title.
E840.8.K4R584 1983   973.922'092'4 [B] 83-15859
ISBN 0-8283-1890-5

Branden Press Inc.
21 Station Street
PO Box 843
Brookline Village MA 02147

**To Shelley, Imy and Ethel
With Love**
Special thanks to my friend John R. McBride
for his help and advice on the manuscript.

Table of Contents

Robert Francis Kennedy

Biography

of a Compulsive Politician

THE ATTORNEY GENERAL AND THE PRESIDENT

Chapter 1
Friday — November 22, 1963

November 22, 1963 was unusually warm for the time of the year. Attorney General Robert Francis Kennedy was having lunch on the patio of his house in McLean, Virginia, with Robert Morgenthau, U.S. Attorney for the Southern District of New York, and Silvio Mollo, his chief deputy. They were discussing a paper on the crime syndicate prepared by the staff of the Justice Department.

Since it was Friday, Bobby's wife, Ethel, served clam chowder and tuna fish sandwiches.

At 1:15 p.m. a maid unexpectedly announced that J. Edgar Hoover was on the phone. At that same moment, a workman dressed in coveralls appeared in the doorway and exclaimed: "It says on the radio that the President has been shot."

On the phone with Hoover, Bobby suddenly brought his hand spasmodically to his grief-stricken face. Realizing the tragedy, Ethel rushed to his side and put her arm around him. For the the next few seconds, he did not utter a sound. At long last, and incredulous, he said: "Jack's been shot. It may be fatal!"

He lumbered out of his chair and shuffled across the patio. Asking Ethel not to follow him, he walked up to an upstairs room where he picked up a telephone to hear Captain Tarzell Shepard, the President's Naval Aide, confirm the news. Downstairs on the patio, with expressions of deep concern, the two guests excused themselves.

"Oh, he's dead," Bobby whispered. He walked downstairs into the living room where several of his friends watched TV.

"He died," he muttered, and then stumbled outside the room, finding his way towards the swimming pool. A few minutes later the phone near the pool rang. It was Hoover again: The President had indeed been murdered in Dallas. The message was terse, for Hoover made no attempt to extend his sympathies; his voice did not indicate he was disturbed by what had happened. Hoover disliked the Kennedys because they were politically liberal.

Bobby began pacing back and forth across the lawn, his head bowed, his hands in his pockets. Browmis, his faithful black Newfoundland dog, trotted behind.

Dean Markham, together with a White House aide and Ethel, soon joined him. Bobby asked them to get the children from the three different schools; then telephoned his brother-in-laws, Sargent Shriver and Stephen Smith, to attend to the necessary funeral arrangements.

Late in the afternoon, friends began to arrive in greater numbers, not realizing that instead of easing his grief they were taxing his nerves. When one found it difficult to express his feelings, Bobby asked:

"How are you doing?"

"I've had better days," the friend replied.

"Don't be so gloomy. It's one thing I don't need right now."

He began to think about his father, an invalid for the past two years as a result of a stroke on a Florida golf course. Joseph P. Kennedy could neither walk nor barely talk. Bobby asked himself how his father would react to the news of his son's murder. After reflecting a bit, he asked his brother, Edward (Teddy), his sister Eunice, and her husband, Sargent Shriver, to go to the family compound at Hyannis Port.

By that time, most of the Kennedys knew what had happened. Returning from a game of golf, the mother of the clan — Rose — found Ann Gargan, her niece and constant companion of the elder Kennedy, rushing toward her with tears streaming down her face.

Inside, Joe Sr. was having his noon-time siesta. Instead of wakening him, Rose phoned the family doctor for advice. Assured that Joe would be able to take the news, she nevertheless waited until morning.

Rose was attending the second Mass at St. Francis Xavier Church when she saw Teddy and Shriver arrive for the eight o'clock Mass.

Later, at home, Joe sat down for his breakfast. Noticing that The New York Times was not in its customary place, he began to suspect something was wrong, but did not say anything. After eating his meal, he took a short swim; then went back to his room to watch television. Glancing at Eunice, Teddy told his father the set was out of order. When the old man saw the cord out of the socket, he asked what was going on. Teddy dutifully connected the set, but quickly pulled the cord out again. Looking deep into his father's eyes, he told him that his son, John Fitzgerald Kennedy, President of the United States, had been murdered. Startled, the old man began to weep. Then he asked Teddy to turn on the television. For the rest of the day he sat there glued to the set.

In Washington, Bobby sat on the lawn with his children. When he told them their uncle Jack was dead, seven-year old David wept bitterly and cuddled close to his father.

The most difficult task completed, Bobby walked to the house and resumed his telephone calls. While on the phone with the new President, Lyndon B. Johnson, who was still in Dallas, Bobby was asked by Johnson if he should have the Oath of Office administered in Dallas.

It is ironic to note that Johnson chose Federal Judge Sarah Hughes to administer the Oath, the same woman who had been turned down for that job by Bobby because, supposedly, she was too old— an act Johnson took as a personal affront. The late Sam Rayburn, Speaker of the House, had prevailed on Bobby to give the 64-year old judge the appointment to no avail.

After phoning his mother twice, he began pacing across the lawn again. He was dressed in gray slacks and a green sweater, and Ethel gave him a pair of dark glasses to cover his red-rimmed eyes.

"Now I have to help Jackie,"he said.

At five in the afternoon, he drove to the Pentagon to see Robert McNamara. After a conversation of about twenty minutes, they took a helicopter to Andrews Air Force Field to await the arrival of Air Force 1 with the body of the slain President.

Against a setting sun, the big plane approached the field. On seeing it, Bobby could barely restrain himself as he rushed forward. When the plane stopped, Bobby ran up the steps onto the ramp, and sped the entire length. On seeing Jackie, he took her into his arms. Overwhelmed and sobbing, she asked, "Will you come with us?"

A yellow lift lowered the coffin. Six men then carried it to the waiting ambulance.

Wearing a blood-stained wool suit, Jackie walked to the ambulance, opened the door and stepped inside. Brigadier General Godfrey McHugh, the Air Force aide, and Bobby followed behind. Sitting on the floor, the three braced themselves as best they could and held their hands on the casket as the car sped away to the hospital.

The Bethesda Hospital Administrators were surprised to see the three arrive with the ambulance, as they were expected to come by helicopter.

Over three-thousand people were waiting outside the hospital. As the casket was carried inside, with the Honor Guard standing tall, the crowed watched in silence.

Jackie sat all night in a suite on the 17th floor of the hospital, her mind preoccupied about the funeral arrangements. She phoned her close friend, the artist William Walton, and asked him to get a book from the White House library. It contained sketches and pictures of Abraham Lincoln lying in state. She also told Arthur Schlesinger, Jr. and Richard Goodwin of the Peace Corps, to go to the Library of Congress and examine a number of books containing facts on procedures for the buriel of the Great Emancipator.

After Jackie slipped into a restless sleep, Bobby and McNamara drove to Arlington Cemetery and picked a grave site near the tomb of the Unknown Soldier.

At 4:42 AM Saturday, November 23, a gray Navy ambulance drove up to the northeast gate of the White House, carrying the body of John FitzGerald Kennedy. Nearby, six cars filled with relatives and friends stood by. A squad of marines met the ambulance at the gate to begin the long procession flowing under the majestic tree-lined driveway. The marines marched in two files, holding their bayonets across their chests at port arms, halting for a few moments when they reached the portico of the White House. There, they were joined by other soldiers, sailors and airmen.

Still wearing her blood-stained suit, Jackie was first to get out of the car. With his arm around her, Bobby walked alongside as the coffin was carried into the East Room where it was placed on a black catafalque— identical to the one that had borne the body of Lincoln. At 4:28 AM, Jackie and Bobby left the room, returning at 10:30 AM with about seventy-five relatives and friends for the private Mass conducted by the Reverend John J. Cavanaugh, the former President of Notre Dame University.

On November 24, the body of the President was moved from the White House to the Capitol Rotunda. Jackie, Bobby, President and Mrs. Johnson followed the solemn procession in a black limousine. When the casket was mounted on the black catafalque, Jackie and her children, Caroline, and John, John, walked up to it and knelt down. Jackie kissed the flag draped around the coffin while Caroline touched it lightly.

Bobby entered the Rotunda to join Jackie and Ted. They knelt near the coffin for a few minutes, then backed away. After turning around, they walked down from the Capitol to the East Plaza.

At the North Portico, a choir of midshipmen was singing softly. Jackie stood behind the caisson with Bobby at her right and Teddy at her left as the procession wended its way towards St. Matthews Roman Catholic Cathedral.

Cardinal Richard Cushing of Boston, an intimate friend of the Kennedys, began to intone the Pontifical Low Mass.

"May the martyrs receive you at your coming. May the spirit of God embrace you, and mayest thou, with all those who made the supreme sacrifice of dying for others, receive eternal rest and peace, Amen."

Jackie, Bobby and Teddy received holy communion.

The Most Reverend Philip M. Hannan, Auxiliary Bishop of Washington, delivered the sermon, quoting the late President's favorite chapter from Ecclesiastes: "There is an appointed time for everything... a time to be born and a time to die... a time to love and a time to hate... a time of war and a time of peace..."

The casket was carried into the bright, clear sunlight outside the Cathedral and placed on a caisson. The procession moved slowly past the Lincoln Memorial, over the Memorial Bridge to Arlington National Cemetary. Bagpipers lead the march and played *The Mist Covered the Mountain,* a favorite tune of President Kennedy.

Numb with grief, Jackie started to walk towards the open grave. Bobby took hold of her arm and guided her to her seat.

Cardinal Cushing intoned the liturgy, speaking about that "wonderful man *Jack* Kennedy." Overhead, fifty jets representing the Union streaked by; on the ground, riflemen fired a three-round volley. While a bugler played Taps, other servicemen lifted the flag from the coffin and gave it to Jackie. Together with Bobby and Ted, she then fed the torch to the eternal light.

Throughout the ceremony, Jackie kept her face covered with a dark veil. When she turned to General Maxwell D. Taylor, she lifted her veil slightly and touched her cheek to his; then reached and took a firm hold of Bobby's hand.

The Lord's Prayer having been recited, the ceremony was concluded. At 3:34 PM, the slain President was finally at peace, lying among the heroes of his great nation.

Being the eldest living son of Joseph P. Kennedy, Bobby was now the titular head of the Kennedy clan. In not too distant future, he would be called to assume the role his father had already vested in his two older brothers. How the two brothers had died jolted Bobby with pain. This elevation by death yielded little satisfaction. He longed for his *Jack* with whom he

5

had always been very close and to whom he gave a loyalty beyond question.

Loyalty was a family trait. A friend once remarked that the clan always bunched up like a herd of bisons, heads lowered as if they were being attacked by wolves, whenever an outsider thwarted the ambitions of any one of them.

For the next several months, Bobby appeared to be lost in grief and incapable of asserting himself. The second most powerful political personality in the nation, suddenly his future became uncertain. He had lost his clout where it counted. At the same time, he was painfully aware about Johnson's feelings toward him, admitting to himself that he did not have much regard for the tall Texan. A vast gulf separated them, and Bobby would soon learn there would be no place for him in the new administration. For a brief moment, he nurtured a hope there might develop a mutual understanding. But it was to prove a forlon hope. Their chemistry simply did not mix. And while they attempted to appear cordial in public, in private they made no secret of their distaste for one another.

Chapter 2
Joe Kennedy And The Making
Of The Dynasty

The saga of the Kennedy clan had its start in Boston in the middle of the 19th century, with Patrick Kennedy. A businessman and ward politician, he was dignified and soft-spoken, wise enough not to drink away his profits. By dint of his temperance and drive, he became a potent force in a city dominated by Protestant Brahmins, where many Irish were employed as domestics and stevedores, or in other menial jobs. A successful saloonkeeper, he was elected five consecutive times to the state legislature, besides being a fire and election commissioner. He could have achieved higher office but he preferred being behind-the-scene.

He became the owner of three saloons, a wholesale liquor company, and a coal business; he was also a major stockholder in the Columbia Trust. By the time Joseph was born (September 6, 1888) Patrick had become one of the most powerful business and political figures in Boston.

He enrolled Joseph in the church of the Assumption Parochial School, transfering him from grade seven there to the Boston Latin School, a highly-regarded public institution. This unusual and bold step was harshly criticised by his patrons and friends. But Patrick knew what was good for his son, Joseph. Being parochial did not necessarily mean being the best. In his book, *The American Irish*, William Shannon said that "The Irish generally saw this move as a sellout or surrender to the hated Yankees." An excellent student, Joseph became president of the senior class and a colonel in the school regiment, having also received the Mayor's cup from the hands of his future father-in-law, Mayor John F. *(Honey Fitz)* Fitzgerald.

In the Boston Latin Year Book of 1908, an anonymous but clairvoyant writer prophesied that Joseph Kennedy would make his fortune "in a roundabout way."

While at Harvard University, together with a classmate he set up a sightseeing bus business at Boston's South Station. His job was to harangue the tourists into buying tickets for tours of the city's historic landmarks. Within months, the two cleared $5,000— a feat not accomplished just through hard work.

Drew Pearson, the Washington, D.C. columnist, revealed that Joe's firm had a potent competitor in the Colonial Auto-Sightseeing Company, which went out of business as a result of an unexpected increase in its license fee from $2,000 to $3,000. It was said that Mayor John F. Fitzgerald, a political colleague of Joe's father, had ordered the increase.

According to Pearson, this fashionably-dressed young Harvard student walked into the office of the Colonial Auto-Sightseeing Company at regular intervals to collect the checks.

"Here's your filthy lucre," an irate bookkeeper would say.

"Friend, it may be filthy lucre, but you'll take note that I take the filthy lucre and put it in my pocket. Good day to you."

Pearson identified him as Joe Kennedy.

Even at that early date, intimates of the Kennedy family said that Joe was out to create a dynasty by making a great deal of money which, in turn, would give him power.

Boston was an unusual place when Joe graduated from Harvard in 1912. It had been the financial center of the nation for many decades, but was losing its supremacy to New York, thanks to the staid and smug Yankees, satisfied to live off the dividends of their blue chips. In the afternoon of Boston's economic greatness, the Irish struggled mightily for a small patch of sunlight.

A sensitive young man, Joe was never asked to join any of the Yankee-dominated clubs. Although the Brahmins allowed a few Irishmen to enroll at Harvard, they did not want them cluttering up their exclusive clubs. The scions of the Cabots—themselves of Italian lineage, — the Lodges, Peabodys, and the other members of the exalted families were invited to come to the social events on Beacon Hill, but Joe and his friends had no other recourse than to go to vaudeville shows or to Irish-sponsored affairs for their amusement.

Joe believed he gained a good deal in going to Harvard where he had managed to make good business contacts, having become a member of the Hasty Pudding, D.F.E., the Institute of 1770 and DU (where he was pledged, along with such future luminaries as Robert Benchley and Clarence B. Randall, who later became a leading industrialist. But the feeling that he was being discriminated against stayed with him throughout his life.

Joe majored in history and economics and made passable grades in both subjects, even winning a varsity letter.

He once persuaded the coach to let him play the final inning against Yale. Harvard had a commanding lead. With few seconds remaining, the captain called time out to put Joe on the field. Luck would have it that he caught the last ball to end the game.

When the players walked off the field, the team captain, who had been responsible for Joe getting the varsity letter, asked him to give him the ball. Joe ignored him and walked off holding tight to it.

Joe set out to earn money. Cash on the barrel-head broke down the social barriers maintained by the Boston Brahmins. He helped his father gain control of the Columbia Trust Company with capital assets of about $200,00, its clientele mainly Irish in search of loans. Sentiment did not get in their way when the Kennedys had to foreclose on the house of a poor Irishman unable to meet mortgage payments.

Utilizing his father's political connections, Joe had himself appointed bank examiner for the State, so he could see the books of the other financial institutions. Of course, the Yankee financiers did not like having an Irishman pouring over their books, but could do nothing to stop him, all being quite legal.

In 1913, there were many bank mergers, a situation presenting serious threats to the older Kennedy and his cohorts, afraid of a Yankee takeover. First National had in fact planned to acquire the Trust Company— but over Joe's dead body. He quickly raised $45,000 from friends, plus an additional sum from the Merchant Bank, and $1,200,000 from Henry J. O'Hara, enough to keep his bank from the Yanks. Then he gave it his *coup de grace* by having himself appointed president.

For a number of years, newspapers throughout the nation kept referring to him as the youngest bank president in the United States, a phrase that irritated him. 'Youth is neither a crime nor a novelty," he once told a reporter.

During this time, Joe began to court the very attractive Rose Fitzgerald, daughter of Mayor Fitzgerald. The Mayor was a five-foot two bundle of energy and blarney, whose chief claim to fame was his unorthodox rendition of *Sweet Adeline*. With it he even enchanted thousands of South Americans who called him *dulce Adelina*.

Rose and Joseph were married in October, 1914 in a ceremony conducted by Cardinal O'Connell.

While the two loved each other, there was very little

empathy between Patrick and Mayor *Honey Fitz.* The serious-minded Patrick considered the peppery little mayor to be more the clown than a leader.

The Mayor, on the other hand, did not relish having a Kennedy as his son-in-law, preferring she marry a certain wealthy building contractor.

But *Honey Fitz* in a way was a failure. He ran for the U.S. Senate and lost; he tried to get elected governor and was defeated, in spite of his ebulliency and appeal to the Americans of Italian descent that his name originally was *Geraldini.*

Mayor James A. Curley, the *Purple Shamrock,* in his autobiography, *I'd Do It Again,* said that his students in civics, especially those who had recently arrived in Boston from Ireland, thought that *Honey Fitz* was the President of the United States and that the laws of the Commonwealth of Massachusetts were made him.

Although it is difficult to tell who of his grandchildren inherited his traits, it seems certain that Rose did not. A devout Roman Catholic, she studied at the Sacred Heart Academy in New York, and at a convent in Europe where she learned French. In Boston, she met regularly with friends to discuss literature and other cultural subjects—in French.

The union of Rose Fitzgerald and Joe Kennedy kindled a dynastic dream in the new husband. As a result, he began to forge lasting connections in the dominant Yankee business and financial community. Armed with enough gall for a regiment of soldiers, he won a solid nitch for himself when he became a member of the exclusive board of Trustees of the Massachusetts Electric company. When his friend James A. Frank asked why he persisted in his endeavor to get on the Board after so many rebuffs, Joe answered:

"Do you know of any better way to meet a Saltonstall and other people of that kind?"

One of his new contacts, a lawyer named Guy Carrier, told Charles Schwab, the steel magnate, to hire Joe as assistant manager of the Bethlehem Fore River Yard in Quincy during World War I. Joe quickly accepted, with a salary of $20,000 a year plus various special bonuses. The shipyard employed about 55,000 workers. When Joe realized there was no restaurant, he promptly created one, baptising it the *Victory Luncheon* as many as 22,000 patriotic workers daily went there to consume their meals.

At this time he met Franklin D. Roosevelt, then Assistant Secretary of the Navy, with whom he had a severe conflict: the

Argentine Government had ordered a number of ships which Joe refused to deliver because of a demand from the embattled Allies, forcing Roosevelt to order Navy tugs to tow the ships out of the yard.

After the war, Joe looked for other businesses. Planning to go into private shipbuilding, he attempted to contact the elusive and hard to reach Galen Stone, Chairman of the Board of Atlantic, Gulf and West Indies, hoping that Stone would give him a start. On learning that Stone traveled daily on the New York to Boston train, Joe cornered him on the train only to be turned down. Stone, however, was so impressed with Joe's audacity that he offered him a job and a salary of $10,00 in a Boston office. In accepting a reduced salary, he knew he would more than make up for it by learning about the brokerage business.

An apt pupil, he acquired great skills as a manipulator; more importantly, he learned to assess the opinions of others. When he became interested in the Florida land boom and was about to invest in it, Stone and Matt Brush told him not to do it.

"Any man can be wrong, but Galen Stone and Matt Brush can't be wrong at the same time," Joe later told a friend.

Soon after resigning his job, however, he bought an enormous amount of Florida land for a song.

In 1922, Joe leased a private office from Hayden Stone at 87 Milk Street. The sign on the door read: Joseph P. Kennedy, Banker. Now, at thirty four, he could operate alone.

Analyzing the *bulls* and the *bears* in the jungle of Wall Street, he learned that killing off business competitors was all in a day's work, there being no Security and Exchange Commission at the time to keep an eye on what went on. Brokerage houses were more like bookmaking establishments and the lack of scruples on the part of the brokers was in keeping with the times. Joe Kennedy was recognized as one of the most astute of the brokers on the little street that starts at the river and ends at a graveyard.

With the active assistance of a few cooperative souls, Joe would buy options on huge numbers of shares and then start creating a public awareness of the stock by selling the paper with the assistance of brokerage houses all over the country. The frenzied activity of the stock duly recorded on the tape tantalized the unwary into buying. When the stock reached a certain *high*, the pool operators would sell at a tremendous profit, creating the inevitable slide. The boys on the inside would be well out of it, but the public— well, it would be caught with a lot of inflated stock.

Excessive speculation in stocks proved to be a wear on Joe's nerves. By the time his sixth child was born, Joe had painful neuritis and stomach ulcers.

Just before the birth of that child, Joe received a phone call from John D. Hertz, President of the Yellow Cab Company, requesting help to fight off a bear raid on his company. Hertz borrowed five-million dollars from his friends Wrigley and Albert Lasker, which he planned to use as an operating fund. Instead, he gave the money to Joe, who established himself in a room at the Waldorf-Astoria Hotel where he began to phone key men over the country. After a series of maneuvers, he was able to steady the stock of Yellow Cab and whip the *bears*. He had not stirred out of his room for four weeks, leaving it only to see his new infant daughter, and only after he had successfully achieved his goal.

A few months later the stock market plunged, thus dooming the Yellow Cab Company with its poor earning report. Suspicious of Joe, Hertz thought that Joe had undermined the foundation with his stock deals. But the accusation was unwarranted.

While still busy with his Wall Street operations, Joe developed an interest in the movie business. In time, he gained a controlling interest in the Robertston-Cole Studios and the Film Booking Office of America. As a result, he moved to New York.

Despite his successes, he was still rejected for membership in the exclusive Cohasset Country Club. His attractive daughters were not invited to join the ultra-exclusive clubs patronized by the Yankees.

Joseph McCarthy, author and friend of the Kennedys, was told by Joe that it made no difference when his daughters were snubbed by the Beacon Hill denizens, saying that his "girls would not have joined, because they never gave two cents for that society stuff." His remark had a hollow, hurt ring to it.

As a motion picture producer, Joe got off to a fast start, producing horse operas and class "d" features with such renown thesbians as Fred Thompson and Red Grange, the All-American football star. Joe ground them out at the rate of one movie a week, with budgets running to $20,000 each. The flood of money poured in at such a great rate that it made his Wall Street earnings appear a Piker's dream. But, although he was having a gay time in Hollywood, he was not at peace with himself.

Just as he was reaching for the stars, he saw a blight striking fairyland. It struck like a plague of locusts in a wheat field.

When Warner Brothers brought out *The Jazz Singer*, the first talkie, they threw the local masterminds into a frenzie, with the careers of squeeky-voice male and raspy-voice female sexpots vanishing with the snows of yesteryear together with their expensively manufactured silent flicks suddenly all becoming obsolete.

The Radio Corporation of America had moved into the movie business at a very late date, its directors deciding to purchase a chain of theaters and, thusly, control the market with the firm's Photophone patents. The handwriting on the wall, Joe sold many of his theaters to RCA in a deal comsumated with David Sarnoff in a New York restaurant at high noon.

Riding high as a producer, Joe engaged his good friend—, Gloria Swanson, to star in some of his films which made fabulous profits. However, Joe made a serious mistake. He engaged Erich von Stroheim to direct one of his more ambitious undertakings.

The Queen Kelley starred Gloria as the movie's blockbuster. Though the original script wasn't all that bad, by the time von Stroheim was through doctoring it, the story made no sense.

Among other things, von Stroheim planned to shoot a scene in which the madame of the bordellos was to receive the last rites of the Catholic Church from her lover, a priest. Fed up by this and other scenes, Gloria flounced off the set and telephoned Joe in Palm Beach. Enraged, he fired von Stroheim and got somebody else to finish the film.

Although *Queen Kelley* ended being a dud artistically and financially, Joe was able to recuperate most of his losses with *The Trespasser*, which also starred Gloria Swanson, with whom Joe had more than a passing relationship.

By October, 1928, Joe was head of two motion picture companies and had control of the Keith vaudeville circuit, earning about $6,000 a week. In addition, he collected a tidy sum in stock options. A few months later he arranged a merger of F.O.B. with Keith Orpheum and sold his stock in the enterprise for five-million dollars for which he received a bonus of about $150,000.

Years after his Hollywood activities had terminated, he returned to lecture to his former fellow-producers. In the first volume of Harold Ickes' *Secret Diaries*, the late Secretary of the Interior wrote that Joe delivered a speech to several hundred of Hollywood's most prominent producers and predicted the defeat of Great Britain by the Nazis. Ickes also stated that Joe was about to start an appeasement campaign to convince Roy Howard of the Scripps-Howard chain of newspapers; Joe Patterson, publisher of the *New York Daily News,* and William Randolph Hearst were also asked to join in his crusade to keep America out of the war.

According to Ben Hecht, Joe even cautioned Jewish producers to stop their protests against the German atrocities for fear they would create an impression that the United States was fighting in a war to save Jews.

Telling a friend that "only a fool holds out for the top dollar," Joe liquidated his holdings in stocks just before the collapse of 1929.

Financially secure, he began to entertain visions of becoming a power in national politics, having often discussed domestic and world politics at home. Like the renowned autocrat at the breakfast table, Joe conducted lengthy sessions on politics while his children munched their food. Joe often asked his first son, Joe Jr., to voice his opinions; then he would turn to *Jack* while the girls, together with little Bobby and Teddy, would sit to listen.

Joe saw his chance to jump into national political life when Franklin D. Roosevelt announced his candidacy for the Presidency.

Besides contributing $25,000 to the campaign and a loan of $100,000 to the Party, Joe also worked hard during the campaign, traveling all over the country with the candidate. After the election, Joe waited patiently for his reward, which was not forthcoming. Finally, President Roosevelt considered offering Joe a cabinet post as Secretary of Commerce, but Louis McHenry How recommended against it. Unsuccessful with the President, Joe tried to use his influence on young James Roosevelt to get himself connected with the leading British distillers of Haig and Haig, King William Whiskey, John Dewar Scotch and Gordon's Gin.

When James Roosevelt asked to be cut in on the deal, Joe replied: "You can't do that; it would embarrass your father."

Not long after that episode, Joe tried to see the President, causing many to marvel at the nerve of this Irishman. But Joe's elephant-like hide was as tough as ever. Those same people were more surprised when the President asked Joe to head up the newly created Security and Exchange Commission. With this new position, Joe became the officially designated policeman over the *bears* and the *bulls.* New Dealers were furious and indignant.

By making the Wall Street operators toe the line, Joe quickly achieved success and respect, especially from the President, who visited him frequently at his new Maryland estate where they drank together and watched the latest movies.

Joe had a passion for Beethoven and Mozart. When his pals objected to this music, he shouted, "You bastards don't appreciate culture."

Resigning his Commission in 1935, he undertook a special assignment from David Sarnoff and Hearst to make a study of their companies, at $10,000 a week from Hearst alone. But making money bored him, his hunger being for political power. He volunteered to campaign for Roosevelt; this time he was rewarded with a job as Chairman of the Maritime Commission. In a short period of time, he pulled all the ship owners into line. Later he recalled one incident:

"I had a hunch that this boy was trying to razzle-dazzle us into giving him something for nothing. So I called him in [and] told him his claim wasn't worth a cent, and we'd fight any suit he brought for any amount and when he swallowed that and settled for nothing I knew he'd been trying to razzle-dazzle us."

Joe was equally firm with labor leaders. When big Joe Curran, chieftain of the CIO Maritime Union, walked into Joe Kennedy's office, the smaller Joe got up and rushed the bigger man right out of his office. He then telephoned Frances Perkins, Secretary of Labor, telling her that her "sweetheart was just in here."

"Curran is a nice boy," she reported.

"Not in my book, he's not," he retorted, "and don't send any more bums like that in here trying to tell me what my authority is."

His historic moment came, however, when Roosevelt appointed him the U.S. Ambassador to the Court of St. James: he, an Irish Catholic representing the United States of America—in England's capital of all places. Because of his refreshingly different ways, he soon found British newspaper columnists dubbing him "*Jolly* Joe, the Nine Child Wonder."

Living in grand style, he hired twenty servants plus three chauffeurs. When he entertained, he added twenty more domestics. And, of course, all the comings and goings were carefully reported in the British press. On the surface, Joe became indeed the most popular U.S. Ambassador to London, all the while believing that Germany would win the war and that France and England would "go to hell," his sole interest to save enough money for his children. He even criticized Roosevelt on this issue. When Bullitt accused him of being disloyal to the Chief Executive, Joe replied that he would say £what he God-damned pleased to whom he God-damned pleases."

When word reached the White House, the President decided that "the young man needs his wrists slapped."

An advocate of appeasement, Joe was a most intimate friend with Sir Horace Wilson and Sir John Simon, two key appeasers in the Chamberlain cabinet.

A few days after the Munich Pact was signed, Joe delivered a speech at a Trafalgar Day dinner, telling the British that the super-human efforts of Chamberlain on behalf of peace should have the "respect of all of us."

On June 13, 1938, Herbert von Dirksen, the German Ambassador to London, informed his superiors in Berlin that he had met Joe a number of times, that Joe not only was sympathetic towards the Nazi regime, but that he also thought that the German people were happy with Hitler as their Chancellor.

The Washington, D.C. columnist Kenneth Crawford once accused Joe of having used his influence to have certain critical comments about Chamberlain's appeasement policies deleted from a Paramount Newsreel before it was exhibited in England. A national magazine reported that Joe had told columnist Walter Winchell that he had persuaded Colonel Charles A. Linderbergh to give his frightening estimation of the strength of the German air force. This opinion about the Luftwaffe, which he had imparted to Chamberlain, helped him convince the British people that appeasement of Hitler was the only choice for peace.

Winston Churchill and other opposition leaders became increasingly annoyed with Joe, and blamed him for spreading rumors in the U.S. that Churchill did not like Americans.

Joe made a sarcastic remark about King George VI's speech impediment; scoffed about the Queen's taste in clothes, saying that she looked like a housewife but conceding that she was one of the "most intelligent women he had ever met," adding that "she's got more brains than [Chamberlain's] Cabinet..."; lamented that England would "go socialist"; and predicted that "if the United States gets into [the war] with England we'll be left holding the bag." He further told Lyons that he planned to meet with William Randolph Hearst to discuss ways to create public sentiment against any U.S. involvement in the war, pointing out that "our Congressmen are dopes and don't understand the war or our relationship to it." He also said that the

British had not taken "over the Irish ports because of American public opinion," but neglected to report that the Germans were spying on the movement of British ships.

"England [doesn't] have a Chinaman's chance of beating Germany..." Joe belabored, adding that "if Hitler lost the War, chaos and communism would follow as a natural consequence of his defeat."

The story, written by Louis Lyons, was published in the *Boston Globe*. It hit Washington with the force of a raging hurricane. Joe tried his best to explain away the entire episode, accusing the reporter of having violated a confidence in revealing his thoughts on world politics, stating that the interview was supposed to be off the record. But Lyons insisted it was quite to the contrary.

Joe was recalled, and with it went his secret ambition to run for President of the United States. Beaten but not defeated, he forged a weapon unique in the 20th century national politics: he established the Kennedy Dynasty.

Through his sons he planned to achieve the ultimate power—the natural extension of his own super-ego, a charge he imparted to all of his children, especially the boys, first Joe., then *Jack,* then Bobby, finally Teddy, and their children and children's children.

"He wasn't around much as some others when the kids were young," commented one of them, "but, whether he was there or not, he made his children feel that they were the most important things in the world to him. He was terribly interested in what they were doing. He held up standards and was very tough when we failed to meet them. The toughness was important. If it hadn't been for that, Teddy might be just a playboy today. But he exercised his authority at a crucial period in his life and this brought out in Teddy the discipline and seriousness which made him an important political figure he is today."

The children respected their father's political opinions, especially the boys who went along with his conservative leanings during their younger days. Strangely enough, (aside from Bobby, who went on to become a compulsive politician like his father) when they got older, first John, then Bobby, and finally Ted all took the liberal road. Old Joe did not object to their political opinions because he understood that power was the name of the game, and it came whether one was liberal or conservative. What each son had to do was to pursue it thoroughly and completely.

17

Chapter 3

Joe Assures The Succession

Despite his toughness in the world of men, Joe Kennedy was a loving father, aware of their importance in his plans, cherishing them, nurturing them, helping through encouragement, and always directing them.

Rose, on the other hand, was the perfect partner. When Joe was away, she took care of their discipline, their physical and spiritual well-being, keeping an index card on their illnesses, dental work and other details.

Joe Jr. became his father's right arm, especially when away from home. Known as a bully, Joe Jr. was his father's favorite. When the Patriarch was away, he assumed the role of the father. As a result, he came into frequent conflict with his brothers, especially with *Jack*. Bobby recalled one frightening incident when he and his sisters cowered in an upstairs room while the two brothers fought in the hall, hitting each other as much as possible.

Joe invested his most deep-felt ambitions— to have a Kennedy in the White House— in his Joe, a talented athlete and a good student, but lacking in business acumen. Politically, however, the two were on the same wave length.

In 1940, Joe Jr. was sent as a delegate to the Democratic Convention in chicago. Having pledged to cast his vote for James A. Farley, a conservative— when the motion was made to have Roosevelt nominated by an unanimous vote, Joe Jr. was the only one to hold out. And like his father, he regarded Hitler invincible, thinking that it would be in the best interests of the United States to enter into a barter exchange with Nazi occupied Europe.

Even at home, they complemented each other. A friend described a typical scene: the children had to appear at the table at least five minutes before dinner. Joe made the opening remarks, with Joe Jr. giving his point of view which usually coincided with that of his father. Then *Jack* would speak in his quiet way, and occasionally, the intellectual Kathleen was permitted to voice some opinions. Bobby, on the other hand, was submerged by the older brothers; he had to continuously fight for a little place in the limelight.

Although Joe seldom talked about business, he tried to interest them in making money. He even sent them to work for two weeks a year with the Columbia Trust Company, but to no avail. The boys just did not display any interest in the commercial world. After all, why should they; their father had assured them financial security for the rest of their lives. Later, however, they learned that their father not only had a knack for making money, they also understood that through money they could achieve power.

With the help of Cardinal Francis Spellman, who introduced Joe to John J. Reynolds, a real estate broker and adviser on property for the local diocese of New York, Joe invested money he had recently made from the sale of securities in Manhattan properties whose land values had been depressed from the beginning of the War. Buying buildings and land at bargain prices, Reynolds increased Joe's fortune to over 100 million dollars.

Joe purchased a property located at Fifty-First Street and Lexington Avenue for $600,000 and sold it for $3,000.000. He bought another at Forty-Sixth and Lexington Avenue for $1,700,000 and sold it for $4,975.000. Another at Fifty-Ninth and Lexington Avenue he bought for $100,000 and sold for more than $5,000,000 a few years later.

While Joe was counting his profits, he devised a system to increase his cash. Here's how:

A building cost $2,000,000. With the right contacts, he secured loans for $1,800,000 at low rates. Although the annual interest came to $72,000, rentals amounted to 6% of the price he had paid— a total of $120,000 a year. After deducting the interest due the bank, he was left with a net of $48,000 a year. On his cash investment of $200,000, he was making 24% profit plus the increased value of the building.

Having learned how to put the squeeze on small home owners in Boston, when in New York he applied the same techniques in getting substantial increases in rent from his tenants. The General Welfare Committee received numerous gouging complaints. But there was little anyone do.

Joe's most ambitious real estate undertaking was the purchase of Chicago's Merchandise Mart from Marshall Field and Company, a 24-story building with 93 acres of renting space valued at $21,000,000 in 1945.

After securing favorable mortgage rates, he substantially increased the rents, thus raising the value of that property to about $100,000,000 in no time.

While the War was going on, Joe thrived. His sons, however, joined the services: Joe Jr. enlisted in the Air Force, *Jack* and Bobby in the Navy.

Although Joe Jr. had had more than his share of missions and was due to be sent home, he nevertheless volunteered to fly a PB[-4 Liberator plane loaded with high explosives over the English Channel and to parachute to safety after setting it on its course towards German targets. While in flight, the plane exploded. His body and that of the pilot were never found.

The tragedy had a profound effect on his father. All of his work, his planning and grooming seemed to have gone up in that airborne holocaust. His consolation (if it can be called such) was in his realization that he had three other sons, thus assuring him his succession.

Cultivating John *Jack* Kennedy presented a different challenge. John lacked the lust for power. An author at heart, John wrote an essay, *While England Slept,* during his Harvard years. But with the death of his brother, his secret ambition came to an abrupt end. Although Joe had had other plans, fate would have John fulfill a dream— alas, at a tremendous cost.

Having understood John's lack, Joe moved to remedy it through Bobby, whose lust for power had by now become more evident. Joe worked it so that one brother complemented the other, the key being to make them inseparable. But although Joe fulfilled his plan in getting a Kennedy into the White House, fate was to doom the dream by turning it into tragedy for his family and the nation.

Chapter 4
The Shaping of Bobby

The Kennedys tell many anecdotes about Bobby's childhood, almost all touching on his predominant quality— a tenacity which often turned compulsive.

When he was four years old, Bobby was sailing in a yawl on Nantucket Sound. When Joe Jr. suggested he jump overboard to try to swim, Bobby, who did not know how to swim, quickly obeyed. He almost lost his life, had Joe Jr. did not dragged him out of the water. A few minutes later, and without any warning, Bobby jumped again, and Joe Jr. once again saved his life. So determined was he in learning how to swim and to show that he could do it, that he jumped for the third time, and was about to drown if it hadn't been for his brother's timely rescue.

In telling this story to intimates, President John Kennedy could not make up his mind whether the incident "showed... a lot of guts or no sense at all."

Another interesting incident took place in New York where Joe had purchased an imposing mansion in nearby Bronxville. A tomboy, Eunice liked to indulge in horseplay, frequently wrestling with her brothers. One day, the ever-playful girl tossed a plate of chocolate frosting at Bobby, hitting him squarely in the face to the laughter of all those present. Angered by the embarrassment, Bobby pursued Eunice all over the house. On cornering her, he shut his eyes and charged towards her head on. Eunice sidestepped him, causing Bobby to crash into a table, cutting his head so severely that a doctor had to to stitch the wound. That was not all.

While working in the tool shed, he dropped a radiator on his foot, smashing one of his toes.

At an elegant party, he lifted a goblet of tomato juice with such vigor that he splashed it all over the ceiling, on the table cloth, and on the clothing of many guests. He even accidently spilled tar into his eyes and almost impaired his sight.

Because he wasn't that tall, his strength as an athlete was rather limited. But what he lacked in strength he more than made up in determination. By diligent application, he acquired proficiency in football, baseball, swimming, tennis, cricket, soccer and hiking. At Harvard, he made the varsity football team although his weight at the time was only 160 pounds. He practiced passing, hitting the line and other exercises from early morning until late in the afternoon. Kenneth O'Donnell, his close friend and former teammate, tells the following story:

"He had no right to be on the varsity team. It was just after the war and all the men were back from the service. We had eight ends who were bigger, faster and had been high school stars. But Bobby was a quick, tough guy who worked five times as hard as anybody. He'd come in from his end like a wild Indian. If you were blocking him, you'd knock him down, but he'd be up again after the play. He never let up."

Bobby could endure pain like a Spartan. During one practice session, a tackle kept eluding Bobby with apparent ease. Although the coach ordered the team to repeat the play, Bobby couldn't get within arm's length of the tackle. The coach was raging mad. As he was about to give Bobby a dressing down, Bobby collapsed at his feet: Bobby had been playing with a broken ankle.

The would-be athlete was critical of those not adept at sports. During a touch football game with his brothers and sisters at Hyannis Port, John, who wasn't in good form, missed a pass. Bobby turned to him and told him he had "guts but no brains." That was the last time he took such liberties; on the following day, John became President-elect.

Of all Joe's sons, Bobby was the only one to display abilities as a businessman. There are people in Bronxville who still remember his peddling the *Saturday Evening Post* and *Ladies Home Journal,* canvassing the area for subscriptions with the family chauffeur driving in the Rolls Royce, and accompanied by his pet dog, Porky. Dave, the chauffeur, would stack the magazines in the rear seat while the neophite salesman sat up front. When he got bored, he would have Dave deliver the magazines. Bobby eventually lost money and stopped.

He then turned to raising rabbits out of the toolshed. With this business, however, he made a profit of $42 which he gave to his mother for deposit in the Hyannis Port Bank.

His school attendance was erratic at the private schools of Riverdale and Bronxville, and at the exclusive Gibbs School in London where he had many an argument with the English boys who insisted that England had been chiefly responsible for winning the first World War, whereas Bobby attempted to convince them that the United States was chiefly responsible for winning that conflict— the arguments inevitably ending in fistfights.

With the outbreak of war, Bobby was enrolled at Saint Paul School in Concord, New Hampshire. On learning it was an Episcopalian institution, Rose had him immediately transferred to the Porstmouth Priory of the Benedictines where he stayed for three years, doing his fourth year at Milton Academy.

A classmate said that Bobby "was not good at small talk... no good at social amenities... and not a great lover."

After graduating from the Academy, he spent some time at Bates and later at Bowdoin, receiving his final training as a naval recruit at Harvard.

In 1945, he talked with James Forrestal, Secretary of the Navy and a close friend of his father, asking for assignment to Active Duty. Forrestal made arrangements; in time Bobby was serving on a newly commissioned destroyer, the *Joseph Kennedy Jr.* To his chagrin, the ship was never used in active service; instead, he found himself scraping paint and watching radar blips in the calm and peaceful Caribbean Sea.

His first political opportunity came one year after the war ended. John was about to launch his campaign to represent Boston's Eleventh District in the U.S. Congress. The District included East Boston, the North and West End, Charleston, and Cambridge, including part of Somerville. Though most of the voters were Irish, there were also large groups of Italians and Jews. Because there had been no Republican elected in that district for over fifty years, winning the tough Democratic nomination was tantamount to being elected. That district had been a kind of feudal fief of James M. Curley, who had vacated it to run for Mayor of Boston. As soon as they were told about Curley's plans, the Kennedys rushed forward. Although John conducted the campaign, Bobby, Red Fay, Timothy Reardon and a few college friends helped out. Joe got his cousin Joe Kane, a very experienced politician, to help; it was Kane who proceeded to initiate the young aspirant in the intricacies of Boston politics. To handle the Italian vote, they got the expertise and the help of Luise Raia.

"In politics," Joe Kane said, "you have no friends, only fellow conspirators." He was also responsible for the slogan,"The New Generation Offers A Leader."

Kane was a very clever adviser. He told John to delay announcing his intention until the last moment. By not announcing early, John saved himself money he otherwise would have to pay other candidates to withdraw.

His rivals were Michael F. Neville, Mayor of Cambridge;

John F. Cotter, Curly's secretary; Joseph Russo, and Catherine Falbey, an ex-WAC Major and lawyer. They almost invariably underestimated John F. Kennedy; certain he couldn't win. When they saw he was a serious contender, they resorted to calling him a carpetbagger, advising him to go back to Palm Beach, insinuating that his father had accumulated his money in unsavory ways. Mike Neville walked into the State House press room dangling a 10 dollar bill and wearing a Kennedy button on his breast pocket.

The only one who could have stopped John was Curley. But grandfather *Honey Fitz* took care of that danger by promising to support him in his bid for the mayoralty.

In charge of the campaign in East Cambridge, including three wards considered the Bailiwick of Mike Neville, Bobby and his willing helpers came up with the strategy to route the opposition. They transformed the election campaign into a series of social events, with the Kennedy ladies serving tea, crumpets and rich cakes to the local housewives who were then gently requested to write down their names and addresses on cards. Later, the Kennedy ladies would contact them personally to insure the votes. Of course, a visit from the candidate's sister had people talking for days. On election day, most of the females voted for the young would-be legislator.

After winning the election, the Kennedys gave large parties at the Hotel Commander in Cambridge where Rose and her girls served tea and sandwiches, while Joe and the other members of the family stood in the reviewing lines busy shaking hands. Both Joe and John were delighted with Bobby's accomplishments.

While in Rio de Janeiro—on a trip won for his campaign efforts on behalf of John,— Bobby expressed his amazement at the vast gap between the few rich and the many poor. Lem Billings, his companion, said that Bobby thought "Latin America was ripe for communism." Bobby also said unkind things about the political situation in Argentina under Juan Peron and his wife Evita.

In Chile, Bobby and Billings decided to climb a mountain peak. At the half-way point, Billings had enough and called it a day. Bobby, on the other hand, kept on climbing until he reached the top.

Back at Harvard, he completed his under-graduate studies. Although he did not display unusual talents, he was accepted by the Boston aristocrats. A member of the Hasty Pudding, Spee and Varsity, he was invited to a number of Back Bay social gatherings, but he turned them down, preferring to go to vaudeville shows.

"I didn't go to class very much," he once acknowledged, "but I used to talk and argue a lot about sports and politics.

"At home we always discussed issues and sports. Because of that I had more knowledge than the other students. But in some areas I had no knowledge, and no particular feeling about certain issues. I was for the veterans' housing bill right after the war, but I know more about the issues today and feel more strongly about them."

His close friend, Kenneth O'Donnell, recalled that "in college in those years the guys were older than Bob and he was less sure of himself. He was not a dominant factor in the group. Bob didn't go to social affairs or dances. He went with the common herd. His friends were persons who couldn't scrap twenty-five cents together. Bob was like the rest of us—finding himself."

After graduating, Bobby became an accredited correspondent for the *Boston Post*. He traveled to the Middle East where he covered the Arab-Israel War of 1947, observing that the Jews would win because of their superior "spirit, zest and determination. They were tougher inwardly and outwardly than the Arabs."

He also went to Germany to witness the Berlin Airlift. He tried to get to Hungary but was unable to get a visa. The government thought he was a Catholic and an agent of Cardinal Spellman.

On returning home, he matriculated at the University of Virginia Law School where he proved himself a better student. He made high grades and was active in student affairs. Among other things, he was responsible for the revitalization of the long dormant Student Legal Forum by inviting distinguished guest speakers: his father; his brother, the President of the United States; Thurmond Arnold; William O. Douglas, Supreme Court Justice; Joseph R. McCarthy, U.S. Senator; and Ralph Bunch. The university authorities objected to having Bunch, but Bobby fought them to a standstill.

After graduating from law school, he thought of going into private practice. Instead, he went to work for the Criminal Division of the Department of Justice, a job that kept him closer to John and to many new and influential political friends.

Chapter 5
Bobby And The World Of Joseph McCarthy

During his early days in Washington, Bobby established a solid friendship with Joseph McCarthy, the powerful Republican Senator from Wisconsin, a friendship that started when the Senator addressed the Student Legal Forum. The older Irishman had instantly taken to the younger Irishman, and Bobby responded to the blarney of the legislator, who bore the same first name as his father. Their relationship proved a lasting one even after McCarthy's disgrace, censure and untimely death. Bobby once said that McCarthy "was always nice to me and I never had any personal disputes with him."

At this time, Bobby also met Roy M. Cohn, another young lawyer who, together with G. David Shine, were to achieve national and international notoriety as a result of a trip to Europe in search of subversives. In fact, Cohn was involved with Owen Lattimore, the John Hopkins professor and noted authority on Far Eastern affairs. The professor had been badgered by Senator McCarthy for being a supposed top "Russian agent" and the boss of Alger Hiss, in an espionage ring operating in the State Department. But Lattimore, being defended by former Senator O'Mahoney, was able to clear himself of the charges.

Still employed as a lawyer in the Department of Justice, Bobby undertook to manage his brother's campaign for the Senate, against Henry Cabot Lodge, an individual considered unbeatable by most of the political soothsayers, one who was equally popular among the Irish as with the Yankees, a liberal largely responsible for the nomination of Dwight D. Eisenhower as the Republican candidate for the Presidency. With Eisenhower heading the Republican ticket, Lodge was expected to easily win the election against young Kennedy. Among other factors, however, Lodge did not consider the role of Senator Joseph McCarthy.

In 1952, McCarthy was a frequent visitor at the Hyannis Port Kennedy compound. A good and loyal Republican, he was expected to deliver a few speeches calling for the re-election of Lodge. But, curious as it appears, McCarthy did not deliver one single speech for Lodge.

Joe Kennedy, of course, denied having anything to do with McCarthy's strange behavior, but admitted being a great admirer of the Senator for his continued fight against the Communists.

He also denied ever having been a close friend of McCarthy. But the depth of his feelings for the Senator was unmistakably revealed on another occasion. When Congressman Kennedy's liberal supporters wanted him to make a declaration against McCarthy, Gardner Jackson (an old-line liberal loaned by the CIO to help Kennedy) had prepared a statement to show the Kennedys on Bowdoin Street in Boston. Jackson read the statement to Joe and his cronies and afterwards asked for Joe's endorsement. Joe leaped out of his chair.

"You and your sheeny friends are trying to ruin my son's career," he shouted.

When Jackson saw that Congressman Kennedy did not disagree with his father, he picked up and left without saying another word.

A few days later, Jackson was in the apartment again with John.

"They gave you a bad time, Pat," John remarked.

"How do you explain your father?"

"Just love of family. No! pride of family."

The relationship between McCarthy and Bobby blossomed during the senatorial campaign. While Eisenhower carried Massachusetts by a tremendous majority, Henry Cabot Lodge went down to defeat by a scant 90,000. Joe McCarthy's silence paid off.

With the election of Eisenhower, McCarthy became Chairman of the notorious Permanent Sub-Committee on Investigations, mining in extremis the political gold of red-hunting. Francis Flanagan, a former FBI agent, while serving as the Committee's General Counsel, asked James McInerney, Assistant Attorney General at the Justice Department during the Truman Administration, to recommend Bobby to fill the post of counsel for the minority. Bobby enthusiastically accepted because as he later explained "the investigation of communism was an important domestic issue."

At the beginning Bobby liked working for McCarthy. His relations with Cohn, however, eroded to a point of antagonism.

Bobby scored a *coup* that rankled Cohn. Having received, during the Korean War, sensitive information about Allied trading with Red China and the Soviets, Bobby took the witness stand and declared that in 1952 the following took place:

a)193 vessels registered in the names of 19 countries had made 445 (possibly 600) trips to Red China.

b)85 had flown the flags of the Allies.

c)65 had carried strategic materials to the Soviets.

d)67 were engaged in trading with the enemy.

He further reported that the Wilhemsen Company of Norway was trading with China, stating that nine of its ships were taking material to China and therefore to North Korea; that the Blue Funnel Line, a British Company, had used 28 ships to take cargo to China; that 10 ships of Panamanian registry had carried material to China; that two of these vessels belonged to the French government, whose ships had been purchased at bargain prices from the United States on which it still held a mortgage; that two British-owned vessels had actually been transporting Chinese troops along the coast, disembarking them near Korea; and that a minimum of 162 boats, 100 of which were under British registry, had been taking important material to China during the first three-and-a-half months of 1963.

He then concluded with the following: during 1953, 12 ships from Norway, six from Denmark and Finland, six from Italy, five from Switzerland, four from France, three from the Netherlands, and one each from India, Pakistan, Portugal and Japan had been carrying cargo to China on behalf of North Korea.

Tom Wilhemsen, the president of the Norwegian shipping company, vehemently denied that his vessels had carried war material to Red China. The British Ambassador waxed indignant at the slander. And a spokesman for the Wheelock-Marden Line said that Bobby had distorted the facts to suit his own purposes.

But Senator John McClellan, the conservative Democrat from Arkansas, a member of the Minority on the McCarthy Committee, thought that Bobby had presented a convincing case against the allies. Joe McCarthy of course liked Bobby's testimony. Arthur Krock, *The New York Times* conservative-minded pundit, a friend of the Kennedys, wrote that the investigation was "an example of Congressional investigation at its highest."

But the iconoclastic I. F. Stone wrote that Bobby's actions were an example of McCarthyism at its worse, stating that only two ships were involved in the China traffic: one, the Perico, owned by Wallen and Company of Hong Kong, whose captain admitted transporting 462 unarmed and allegedly sick Reds from Kawngchoun to Canton on June 22, 1961, further claiming that the higher-ups in the Communist army command had warned him that "someone would be shot if he refused"; the other was the Miramar, a Wheelock-Marden ship, under Panamanian registry, which came into the control of the Chinese during the early part of August 1951, transporting troops to Shangai during the early part of June 1952. And that was all there was to the story.

One lonely dissenter giving the facts in the case was not enough to soil the image of the new Sir Lancelot tilting his lance at the hypocritical, freedom-loving British and other Allies. Despite his great triumph, Bobby resigned shortly thereafter.

Life with Cohn had become unbearable. When McCarthy was reluctant to drop Cohn, Bobby decided to take a job with the Hoover Commission.

Years later, when running for Senator, Bobby was interviewed by Edwin Newman, TV newscaster on *Meet The Press*, who insisted on asking Bobby questions about those days:

"Mr. Kennedy, you were at one time connected with the Senate Committee when Joe McCarthy of Wisconsin was on it and that conceivably will cost you some votes in November. What precisely was your connection with the Committee and how did it come about?"

"I worked for Francis Flanagan. I was involved in other matters such as the fact that the government purchased palm oil and put it in tanks. Momentous matters such as this."

In 1952-early '53, Bobby told a different story: "I felt the investigation of communism was an important domestic issue," conveniently forgetting to tell about his grandstand play against the Allies.

Many highly respected lawyers did question Bobby's way of interrogating the witnesses appearing before the Committee. They were lawyers equally severe about the tactics Bobby had employed when Chief Counsel for the Senate Racket Committee. During one hearing a Teamster Union attorney called him "a sadistic little monster." Joseph I. Rauh, representing the late Walter Reuther and the United Automobile Workers Union at the hearings, was more understanding.

"Any abuses were not due to vindictiveness but to [Bobby's] lack of experience. It if sometimes led to abuse of witnesses it also led to witnesses getting away with murder. The technique of questioning is an art and Bobby wasn't experienced in it. He did not know how to go for the jugular."

Other lawyers said that Bobby had had plenty of experience at the Department of Justice and with McCarthy's Committee and should have known how to question witnesses. They felt that he was able and intelligent, but lacked sympathy for people with non-conformist political ideas. They also said that he had no regard for due process.

Before resigning, Bobby told McCarthy that "he was going out of his mind and was going to destroy himself" if he did not rid himself of Cohn and Schine. McCarthy admitted to Bobby that he did not like either of the two men, that he was planning to discharge Schine, and begged Bobby to stay on at least a month. When he saw that McCarthy did not take action, Bobby resigned.

Bobby spent the next eight months working with the Hoover Commission, finding his work pleasant and fruitful. Deep down, however, he missed the thrills and excitement of the McCarthy Committee hearings and longed to return.

Meanwhile, McCarthy elevated Cohn as his Chief Counsel during the summer of 1953, causing John McClellan, Stuart Symington and Henry Jackson to resign from the Committee, resenting the fact that no one had been consulted them.

Bobby returned to the Committee after the three Democrats had made their peace with McCarthy. Cohn, however, remained on the staff.

William Shannon, *The New York Times* editorial board member and an astute student of the Washington scene, in his book, *The American Irish,* stated that McCarthy was a "rogue" and "a rascally, blarneying happy-go-lucky adventurer and a hard man who loved to gamble at dice, poker or the races and was not a man to be trusted where money or truth were concerned." On the other hand, Bobby saw McCarthy being kind to his friends, being led astray by his two sinister "playboys."

Bobby's close association and friendship with McCarthy caused a great deal of embarrassment to John F. Kennedy during his campaign for the Presidency. John could not express his disapproval because Bobby had worked for him and that his father and sisters admired McCarthy.

When James Madigan of *Newsweek Magazine* tried to elicit a more definite statement from John Kennedy during a TV discussion, Bobby became furious; he refused to speak with Madigan for many months to come.

"How could I get up there and denounce Joe McCarthy when my own brother was working for him. It wasn't so much a thing of political liability as it was a personal problem," John told his biographer in 1959.

John Kennedy was sincere in his conviction that he had no use for McCarthy and all of his works. He voted against the confirmation of Robert Lee, a McCarthy-sponsored man for the job with the FCC; he also voted against the appointment of Scott McLeod, another McCarthy-sponsored security chief at the State Department, as an Ambassador to Ireland, and fought vigorously to have Charles Bohlen confirmed as Ambassador to the Soviet Union despite McCarthy's disapproval.

Bobby's burning hatred for Cohn exploded into the open during the questioning of Annie Lee Moss, a black woman employed by the Army Signal Corps. She had been accused of belonging to the Communist Party because Bob Hall had once brought a copy of the *Daily Worker* to her house. Cohn triumphantly declared that the delivery boy was none other than Robert Hall, one of the chief functionaries of the Communist Party in the District of Columbia. She reiterated that the delivery boy was a Negro. Having learned that Bob Hall was white, Bobby asked Mrs. Moss to describe the delivery man once again, to which Senator McClellan dryly observed that there was a difference between a black and a white Mr. Hall. Like a small boy caught stealing cookies, Cohn promised to look into the matter further.

The grand climax finally flared into the open on June 12, 1954 when Cohn openly threatened to get Senator Jackson.

Jackson had ridiculed a plan conceived by Schine, which was to smash the entire international Communist apparatus to bits. It called for high-class call girls to snare the wily Russians into betraying the innermost secrets of the Kremlin to the United States.

Unable to contain his laughter, Jackson poked fun at McCarthy for the concoction, infuriating Cohn, who in turn warned Bobby of a letter written by Senator Jackson recommending a man identified with Communist causes for a federal job.

"Don't make any warnings about Democratic senators," Bobby retorted.

"I'll make any warning to you that I want to, anytime, anywhere," Cohn added angrily.

"Get lost," Bobby answered with a hand motion of dismissal.

It took the Army-McCarthy hearings, which involved Cohn, Schine and others, finally to make many Americans see that McCarthy was a dangerous demagogue intent on destroying the reputation of the military. As a result of the Peress and Zwicker incidents wherein General Zwicker had sanctioned the promotion of Peress— "a Red", Republican Senator Ralph Flanders started a campaign to censure McCarthy for conduct unbecoming a senator, presenting his resolution in the Senate on July 30, 1954. Senator Arthur Watkins, a Mormon from Utah, headed the Select Committee. On December 2, 1954, the Senate censured McCarthy by a vote of 67 to 22.

Despite the exposure of McCarthy as a fraud and an "adventurer," Bobby continued to maintain a great affection for the man. He admitted that McCarthy "was terribly heavy handed" but he "liked him."

Long after McCarthy's death, Bobby admitted that McCarthy had brought the Senate into disrepute for having terrorized witnesses and manipulated facts.

"The whole operation of Cohn and Schine was the core of it," Bobby explained. "To censure him for not appearing before the Privilege Election Committee or because of what he said about the other senators was not significant."

Bobby had been taught to be loyal to relatives and friends. The man from Wisconsin was his friend, regardless.

A prominent Republican perhaps best revealed Bobby's feeling about McCarthy: "The trouble with Bobby Kennedy is that he has never attached as much importance to methods as to ends. To illustrate, I record the following conversation which I had with him in the spring of 1956, another election year, when Senator Joseph McCarthy was still alive and Bobby Kennedy was chief counsel to Senator McClellan's Permanent Investigation Sub Committee. 'The trouble with you Republicans is that you have done away with the very best man your party has,' Bobby said. Who's that? I asked. 'Joe McCarthy!' Bobby answered with emphasis to which I answered, You must be kidding. But Bobby came right back and said, 'I am not kidding. I think so well of the man I made him godfather of one of my children.' Bobby was angry."

Chapter 6
Bobby, Glimco And Beck

Bobby served as Chief Counsel of the Senate Select Committee on Improper Activities in Labor and Management for three years. As a result of his manner in questioning Dave Beck, the supposed corrupt Teamster Union president, many began to criticize Bobby's own tactics.

In their eyes, the McClellan hearings appeared to be more a police action than a legislative body in search of information about corruption in labor unions and business firms.

Bobby was held responsible by legal experts for the Committee's abuse of its powers.

Professor Alexander Bickel of the Yale Law School wrote that "the voice of indignation was almost inaudible, having been rendered hoarse in the efforts to shout down McCartheyism which is the same thing in wolf's clothing."

In the Glimco hearings, examples of violations of the rights of witnesses were also brought out. Bobby announced that he was about to expose the hoodlum control in a number of labor unions.

During the hearings, Bobby emphasized the fact that Glimco had "been arrested 36 times, twice in connection with murders," but never mentioned the fact that Glimco had not been convicted of the crimes.

Bobby had indeed thought he had caught a big fish in Glimco whom he believed represented evil incarnate. The problem was that once Bobby made up his mind that a person was evil, nothing ever made him change his mind.

One of Bobby's investigators testified that Glimco had a cozy understanding with certain individuals in the Chicago Police Department. Through newspaper stories, the public learned that Glimco had been arrested more often than any other so-called public enemy. Bobby had his investigators give the names of people seen with Glimco: "The Waiter," "Little New York," "Cherry Nose," etc.

Others were termed as "another member of the Chicago Syndicate", or close associates of Hoffa. His investigators told the Committee that Glimco had been indicted several years before in Chicago for extortion, that a number of merchants in the Chicago Fulton Street Market had testified before a Federal Grand Jury that they had to make payoffs to Glimco or else be forced to give up their business. Bobby further declared that the businessmen had been threatened with bodily harm if they did not cooperate, but that Glimco had not been convicted because the trial had been delayed for three years. Finally, he told the Committee that all of the witnesses had admitted giving money to Glimco but that the "gifts" were really Christmas presents given in June.

With the assistance of his star investigator, Bobby was able to pyramid the case against the befuddled Glimco, convincing the Committee that Glimco was the virtual kingpin of Local 777, the one who had forced lesser officials to give "kickbacks". He also declared that Glimco had helped himself to $124,000 from the treasury of a taxicab local to finance the defense of the Fulton Street Market extortion trial. Bobby and his associates declared that Glimco had never consulted any of the officers of the union about the disbursement of funds, that Glimco had just helped himself and used the money as he saw fit, reminding the Committee members that in addition the union leader had maintained his girl friend in style with union funds although he was married.

Glimco took the stand again on March 12. The Chief Counsel asked him how he had acquired his citizenship papers. Glimco pleaded the Fifth Amendment. The barrage of questions Bobby hurled at the embattled Glimco had him dizzy. Bobby's questions were in reality conclusions parading in the guise of proven facts. Many of them were based on mere suspicion.

"Then you were indicted... you used these contracts 'The Waiter', 'Little New York' in order to intimidate the witnesses and get them to change their story."

Glimco pleaded the Fifth Amendment.

"Did you ever do anything to help the union membership, one thing?" Bobby shouted. "You don't care anything about yourself and these other people who are gangsters and hoodlums, do you?"

After some difficulty, Glimco found his voice: "I respectfully decline to answer because I honestly believe my answer might tend to incriminate me."

"I agree with you," Bobby retorted. At this junction Chairman McClellan chimed in on Bobby's side.

"You haven't got the guts to, have you, Mr. Glimco!" insisted Bobby after Glimco's renewed use of the Fifth.

Always the willing helper, Senator McClellan contributed his own deathless dialogue to the drama:

"Morally, you are kind of yellow inside are you not? That is the truth of it."

Glimco was not very much impressed by those appeals. He had by now been accused of lacking courage, of being a moral leper, etc. Realizing that only sticks and stones could break his bones, Glimco continued to plead the Fifth Amendment.

After Glimco, Bobby took on David Beck, a most powerful man in the labor movement, highly regarded by individuals in many walks of life. But his reputation vanished in a sea of mud after Bobby got through.

In his *The Enemy Within,* Bobby wrote that Beck had met with such national figures as Dwight D. Eisenhower, that Beck was a university trustee, but that despite the man's reputation, Beck was a crook who had helped himself liberally to union funds. Carmine Bellino, the Committee's chief accountant, found that Beck had taken many hundreds of thousands of dollars out of his union's treasury. Bobby and Bellino subpoenaed the records of Nathan Shefferman, Beck's labor consultant. The records were taken from a vault in the Boulevard National Bank of Chicago.

The two men carefully examined them at the Palmer House for one hour and concluded that "David Beck was a crook, [that] he] was through as a national figure." The documents "we had just been reading provided the evidence that would finish him," Bobby revealed.

When Dave Beck appeared before the Committee, Bobby declared that he felt sorry for the man. "I must confess," Bobby wrote, "that I felt sorry for him. I looked at him and realized that he was a major public figure about to be utterly destroyed before our eyes. I knew the evidence we had uncovered would be overwhelming. I knew from what we had examined and from my conference with him in New York that he had no choice but to plead the Fifth Amendment against self-incrimination. It was no contest now. He couldn't or wouldn't fight back." Those feelings of pity didn't last but five minutes.

Sure of himself, Beck began to dominate the hearings to the dismay of Bobby, who, increasingly disturbed about how the hearings were progressing, said that Beck was indulging himself in long philosophical discourses not germane to the subject.

Seeing his entire case being smothered by the union leader's long-winded orations, Bobby turned tough:

"Did you use union funds to pay for the gardening around your home?"

Beck pleaded the Fourth and Fifth Amendments and even questioned the authority of the Committee to ask that specific question, invoking Articles one and three of the Constitution. Bobby, not at all intimidated by Beck's resorting to the Constitution, kept on insisting that the union leader admit he had taken $320,000 out of the Teamster Union treasury for his own personal use. A very stubborn man, Beck pleaded the Fourth and Fifth again.

"Do you feel that if you gave a truthful answer to this Committee on your taking of $320,000 of union funds that that might tend to incriminate you?" Bobby lead in. Beck agreed that it probably would.

"You feel the same way?" Bobby asked, and Beck repeated that he did.

Bennet Williams, Beck's lawyer, asked that his client's appearance before the Committee be delayed until the trial was been concluded, explaining that if Beck would have to answer questions for the Committee, the same questions could be used against him at his trial thus forcing Beck to convict himself. Williams further explained that Beck had no choice but to continue to plead the Fifth Amendment or be faced with the "cruel choice of helping the government in its criminal case against him by giving it a preview of his defense or enabling it to draw unfavorable inference from his repeated plea of the Fifth."

McClellan and Bobby would not hear of it in spite of the fact that Beck had cited the Fifth 117 times.

"The hearings will continue," McClellan ordered.

On May 16, Beck was recalled to the stand. Meanwhile, Bobby's staff compiled and mimeographed some 52 pages: Beck had misused his authority, his position and trust as President of the International Brotherhood of Teamsters. One copy was given to Beck and several to the reporters. Williams once again asked for a delay of the hearings, moving for postponing, but McClellan denied it because he did not want Beck not to have an opportunity "to deny or explain" the derogatory information released to the public by the Committee.

"The Committee would be failing in proper courtesy and proper consideration of his rights if it did not extend him the the opportunity," McClellan commented with a straight face.

"In that event," Williams said equally polite, "I want most

graciously to decline the courtesy." And Beck had no other alternative than to continue to plead the Fifth.

The Committee's ability to wreck the careers of those summoned to appear lay in the fact that individuals like Beck were not permitted to have their lawyers cross-examine witnesses who testified against them. Far from being an impartial judge, the Chairman acted as prosecutor and judge.

Professor Bickel stated that "this is a hard, hazardous and abhorrnt thing in our society but such is the law and Bobby just managed to stay within it," admitting that such a method of getting at the truth may "sometimes be unavoidable but it is a necessary evil to be tolerated only when necessary."

The problem is that Committee members and Counsel forget the purpose of such hearings which is to formulate legislation based on the facts uncovered, and not to prosecute or become instruments for *destroying* the reputations of individuals.

In his *The Enemy Within,* Bobby says that Glimco and Beck could have stopped pleading the Fifth. Yet, he knew that neither witness could be *selective* in answering questions because once a witness answers any question, he would have to respond to other related ones at his own peril.

Bobby knew that loaded questions and innuendos were unfair, and he accused Senator Carl T. Curtis, Republican from Nebraska, of using these tactics, but conveniently forgot that he did no less during the Committee hearings.

The public may be thoroughly convinced that a Fifth Amendment plea is tantamount to acknowledgment of guilt. However, many innocent men and women have had to plead the Fifth to help prove their innocence.

According to Professor Bickel, no one since McCarthy had done more than Bobby to foster the impression that a plea of the Fifth is the same as a confession of guilt. Bobby made it a practice to force witnesses to plead the Fifth time and again. He would ask them if they believed that such a response would tend to incriminate them. When they said it would, Bobby agreed with them. It became his *leit motive* during many of the Committee hearings.

"The meaning of due process, of the process of accusation and the defense before judges disinterested in the immediate outcome, is that the government suffers itself to conceive it possible that it may be wrong. Bobby's self-assured righteousness is in vivid contrast," Professor Bickel concluded.

Chapter 7
Bobby's First Bout With Hoffa

Edward Bennet Williams, who had served as a counselor for Senator Joe McCarthy, first introduced Bobby to James Hoffa the Teamster Union leader. The two became quite friendly in 1954, frequently lunching together. Shortly after their first meeting, Williams became the chief counsel for the giant Teamster Union and also acted as counsel for David Beck and James Hoffa.

Bobby also became acquainted with Eddie Cheyfitz, Bennet William's law partner. Both lawyers tried to persuade Bobby to get out of government service and join their law firm.

The three maintained friendly relationships. Williams invited Bobby to dinner at his home and Cheyfitz introduced him to the top functionaries of the union, showing Bobby around the very ornate and immense edifice.

On one visit, Cheyfitz discussed the Reuther brothers. A former member of the Communist Party, Cheyfitz told Bobby that he had run across Reuther in Russia in 1933 and expressed his doubts about his current political convictions.

Bobby was the Chief Counsel of the McClellan Committee which was looking into actions of minor government officials, serving in the clothing procurement program division of the military services. Their trail of corruption led to a number of New York gangsters who had been transformed into legitimate manufacturers of army uniforms. A notorious lot, it included, among others, Albert Anastasia—later gunned down in a Manhattan barbershop— Johnny Dio and his brother Tommy, etc.

Through the efforts of Clark Mollenhoff, a reporter investigating crime and corruption in labor unions and management, Bobby learned that the gangsters had wormed their way into the Teamsters Union, and that Beck and Hoffa were responsible for opening the doors to the thugs.

Cheyfitz, who assumed the role of an honest broker, advised Bobby to check into the activities of Frank Brewster, the chief of the Western Conference of Teamsters. Still quite naive about union affairs and union leaders, Bobby did not realize that he was being used by Cheyfitz to get at Beck, to make Hoffa the leader of the Union.

When Beck appeared for the last time before the Committee on May 16, 1957, Bobby noted with obvious satisfaction that the formerly over-confident union leader had become a pitiful wreck of a man. He was, to quote Bobby, a "dead" man.

"All that was needed was someone to push him over and make him lie down as dead men should. The man to do it was available [and] his name was James Riddle Hoffa."

Hoffa was the Frankenstein created by those who did not approve of Beck. In a way, Bobby made possible Hoffa's ascendancy. When Beck was locked up, the field became wide open for the toughest man to take over the power in the union—James Hoffa. It was strange that all of Bobby's efforts to clean up the union should have resulted in propelling Hoffa to the top. Bobby was to learn the hard way that Hoffa represented an even greater danger to honest unionism than Beck ever did.

Sending Hoffa to jail would not be an easy task. The Teamsters Union was served very efficiently by a battery of high-priced lawyers who knew every trick in the book. Bobby hoped that solid evidence would be enough to get Hoffa convicted; he didn't know that smart lawyers can get around the evidence.

Bobby got his first opportunity to get Hoffa when John C. Cheasty, a New York lawyer, phoned him, hinting that he had some startling facts to reveal about Hoffa. In Washington, Cheasty told Bobby that Hoffa had handed him a $1,000 fee as a down payment, with more to come if he managed to get himself on the staff of the McClellan Committee and act as a stool pigeon. Cheasty also met with J. Edgar Hoover and Senator McClellan. They asked him to pretend that he would act as an informer, and gave him a job as an assistant counsel to the Committee on February 14. He then immediately informed Hoffa and his contact man FishBach, who had originally proposed the idea.

Cheasty got his additional pay from Hoffa, which he handed over to the FBI. In return, he gave Hoffa the special documents prepared by the Committee.

Hoffa was happy knowing that his man would keep him informed about the Committee.

On February 19, Cheasty was given the names of four men due to be suspended by the Committee. Instructed by J. Edgar Hoover and Bobby, Cheasty got in touch with Hoffa and told him that he had some very important information. Hoffa directed him to meet later at Seventeenth and I Streets.

A raw wintery day, with snow piled deep on the sidewalks, Cheasty trudged along towards the intersection. There, a number of FBI agents had been staked out, equipped with cameras. Cheasty handed the documents to Hoffa. A few minutes later, Eddie Cheyfitz arrived in his very expensive car. Hoffa got in and went home to have dinner with none other than Bobby.

Hoffa played the role of a tough guy, saying that he was a dangerous man to cross, and hinting that he knew who would be the first witness at the hearings. He even said that the man hailed from Portland, Oregon. Bobby smiled and said nothing.

When the FBI agents arrested Hoffa that night, they found him with the documents still on his person. He was escorted from the DuPont Plaza Hotel to the Federal District Court, where Bobby was waiting. The two men hardly spoke to each other. A half-hour later, Williams walked in to learn why his client had been taken into custody. Bobby made no attempt to enlighten him, supremely confident that he had Hoffa securely boxed in, so much so that he made a wager with a few newspapermen that he would jump off the Capitol dome if Hoffa managed to get himself acquitted. When Hoffa was freed, Bobby attributed the loss to the poor legal work of the lawyers. Others blamed the Negroes serving on the jury, especially Joe Louis, the former heavyweight champion of the world, who appeared as a character witness for Hoffa. Martha Jefferson, a black lawyer, came from California to lend her talents for the simple need to impress the black jurors. A white lawyer from Arkansas was also present; he was a law partner of the presiding judge's brother. The two lawyers even posed for a picture which was published in the *Afro-American* paper together with an advertisement in eulogy of Hoffa for his great affection for the Negro race. Williams even told the jury that Cheasty had at one time investigated the NAACP. It was not true but it startled the jurors.

Bobby took the stand. He rendered a factual account of his meeting with Cheasty and described how the evidence against Hoffa had been procured. Though his testimony was true, it did not convince the jury. Williams was able to transform what was basically a criminal case into a civil rights demonstration, and in the process created a new public image for Hoffa. The union leader now stood before the world as another Martin Luther King. Hoffa had the sympathy of the Negro jurors before he uttered a word. On the stand he swore that he had hired Cheasty to be one of his counselors and that he had never—

hardly ever—asked him to act as a double agent.

Bobby took his defeat in court with apparent good grace. "Under our system of laws," he explained, "if a jury finds a defendant not guilty, he is cleared of the alleged crime. As a citizen and lawyer I accept this, even when I have personal knowledge of the case and feel strongly about the outcome."

Many people questioned whether he meant what he said, recalling his tamperings with due process. In the Hoffa case, however, the characters of a few jurors left much to be desired. Bobby revealed that one of the jurors had been convicted of a number of crimes; another had nine convictions on his record; yet others had been picked up for drunkness and other charges. One was even fired from a government job because of his homosexual practices; another had narcotic connections. Why the staff lawyers at Justice agreed to let such people serve as jurors on so important a case remains a mystery.

Two months later, Hoffa was elected President of the Teamsters Union. A few days after, Williams offered Bobby a parachute; Bobby, however, never took the jump from the dome of the Capitol.

Chapter 8
Bobby vs. Hoffa

Bobby had no intentions of letting Hoffa go scot-free. A new trial was set in Nashville, Tennessee—selected by Bobby because he believed that through the local people he could get a conviction.

Bobby's main witness was Ed Partin, one of Hoffa's union brothers. He had a jail sentence facing him for past crimes. Bobby convinced him to serve as a spy in the Hoffa camp and to act as a "surprise" witness.

Partin was portrayed as an honest, upright, clean-living citizen who, because of his patriotism, had volunteered to appear in court against Hoffa, even if it meant risking his life.

Aware of the tacticts, Hoffa complained to the press:

"Our phones are tapped and our hotel rooms bugged. We'd make remarks just to see what happened and the government attorneys would know what we had said. We are building a new $800,000 headquarters in Detroit and they came to me and said that the whole place is wired and bugged. I said, 'Well, what d'ya expect? Go on and finish building.' They go to school and investigate my kid. He's a good kid, if I say so. They go around to his friends and say, 'How many suits of clothes has Jim Hoffa got? How much money does he carry around in his pocket?' They gave orders to every airline office in the country. When does Hoffa make a reservation? When he calls the FBI office, give our people the time he takes off and the time he arrives. You wouldn't believe some of the creepy stuff they are pulling."

The government, of course, denied bugging Hoffa's office.

When the Test Fleet Trial opened in Nashville in October 1962, Hoffa did not know that one of his trusted henchmen was a witness for the prosecution. Hoffa realized it only two weeks later when Partin appeared in court.

From the very beginning of the trial, about 15 FBI agents were shadowing Hoffa's lawyers. Bobby was simply driving Hoffa to distraction.

"The son of a bitch is killing me," Hoffa complained.

On March 4, the jury finally found Hoffa guilty and he was sentenced to eight years in jail and was given a $10,000 fine. In getting that conviction, however, Bobby had tossed all the rules of Anglo-Saxon jurisprudence out the window. Lawyers who had no regard for Hoffa nevertheless challenged Bobby's methods. And Hoffa, naturally, accused Bobby of having engaged a host of stool pigeons to spy on him, that the government had allocated $600,000 to "railroad him" to jail.

The Civil Liberties Union took up Hoffa's cause, stating that Hoffa's rights had been tampered with and that the due process clause of the Fifth Amendment and the right of counsel had been violated by Bobby.

Planting Partin as the stool pigeon was an "interference." The Union also believed that the article published in *Life* on July 20, 1962, had apparently been timed to create a pre-trial anti-Hoffa climate among the populace.

On May 9, 1964, *Look Magazine* published an article about a plot to murder Bobby. Written by Clark Mollenhoff, it was released just before Hoffa was to stand trial in Chicago.

Bobby's pattern was obvious: first try the culprit in the press; then use every means to obtain a conviction. Despite several failures, his plan finally worked in Nashville.

Chapter 9
The Wisconsin and West Virginia Primaries

In the Wisconsin primary Bobby was the general-in-chief of all operations— a tough man, even vindictive. On hearing a newscaster state that the Kennedys were certain to receive every Catholic vote in the state, he exploded into such a volcanic rage that he frightened everyone within earshot, especially the newsman at the other end of the phone to whom he gave a blistering chewing-out.

Bobby and his colleagues devised a very clever campaign strategy to defeat Hubert Horatio Humphrey.

Ron Mat, a columnist on the *Madison Capitol Times,* said that Governor Gaylord Nelson had checked over a Kennedy poll and discovered that the Massachusetts Senator was leading Humphrey by a large margin.

Joseph Alsop, the well-known Washington birdwatcher, and a very good friend of John F. Kennedy, wrote that Lou Harris, the pollster, had Kennedy ahead by 53% to Humphrey's 47%. The same poll was later repeated in another column by Robert S. Allen and Paul Scott. A third poll had Kennedy up by 57%. Another had 323,00 votes to Kennedy and 242,000 to Humphrey.

"I wonder if these polls are not being used to frighten people out of running for office or into getting aboard someone else's bandwagon," said Elmo Roper in one of his speeches.

Harris, the Kennedy pollster, on the other hand, reiterated that polls were essential tools for the candidates.

During the campaign, Bobby spoke to school children, to farmers, as well as to women's organizations, telling them about Hoffa's misdeeds, how oil barons were contributing huge sums of money to the Humphrey campaign, and that Texas oil moguls were using Humphrey to eliminate Kennedy.

John Kennedy won the election with 479,901 votes to Humphrey's 372,034. Kennedy lost the predominantly Protestant Third, Ninth, and Tenth Districts, but won all those controlled by the McCarthyites.

Now in West Virginia, a mainly Protestant state, Bobby needed to show support for his brother across social and religious lines. To accomplish this, he enlisted Franklin D. Roosevelt, Jr., who immediately accused Humphrey of being a draft dodger:

"There's another candidate in your primary. He's a good Democrat, but I don't know where he was in World War II."

Humphrey had been deferred because he was a teacher, the father of three children, and because he had a double hernia. Some editorial writers found Roosevelt's remarks distasteful and recommended that he be dumped. John Kennedy voiced his displeasure, but admitted later that the statement had helped in winning votes.

"Those boys play both the high road and the low road and they both get splashed. They cannot keep out of each other's ditch," Humphrey commented. "Bobby should examine his conscience about the innuendos and smears. If he has trouble knowing what I mean, I can refresh his memory easily. It is a subject he should not want opened."

But Bobby was not to be intimidated. He traveled all over the state telling the good citizens of West Virginia that Jimmy Hoffa ordered his minions to vote for Humphrey.

Needless to say, John Kennedy won. These two primary victories convinced the power brokers that John Kennedy was indeed the best choice to beat the Republicans in November, and that Bobby was the best campaign manager any candidate could ever want.

Chapter 10

The National Convention

With his 40 liaison men, Bobby planned to keep a firm control over the delegates coming to Los Angeles with their votes. He counted 114 safe ones from the New England states, another 265 from the Northeast, 36 from the Farm Districts, 31 from the Old South, 61 from the Mountain States, 28 from the Pacific Coast, and a few scattered votes from the territories— a total of 550 votes. The only problem was that the votes from Pennsylvania, Illinois and New Jersey were still uncommitted. There were other problems: Governor Lawrence entertained a hope that Stevenson might be chosen as the Party's nominee, Governor Meyner still resented Joe Kennedy's raid for delegates in the northern area of his state, and Boss Daley of Chicago was playing it coy.

The famous Kennedy card file with complete biographical sketches of over 3,200 delegates and alternates was carefully guarded in Suite 8315.

A Kennedy liaison man admitted to Roland Evans, a reporter for the defunct *New York Herald Tribune,* that he was "responsible in precise detail for knowing the political views of every name on the blue cards. There's a secret telephone in the Kennedy headquarters manned around the clock, 24 hours a day. I call that phone every day to make my daily report. An organization man at the other end of the phone has a duplicate card that exactly matches mine. I not only call once a day, but I call the instant that I know of any change in attitude of anyone of the delegates listed on my cards. Immediately, not in five minutes. After reporting the change I note it on my own card."

A network of phones made it possible for headquarters to maintain contact with every liaison man on the floor of the convention. Lines were run from the control post under the floor to phones which had been placed on the seats of the delegates well-disposed towards Kennedy. On the floor, eight men with duo-com walkie-talkies were being directed by Bobby and Governor Ribicoff. A special line linked Suite 8315 to Kennedy's secret hideout in Hollywood. This streamlined communications network became the envy of all the other contenders for the Presidential nomination.

The convention was scheduled July 9 to 13. On Saturday, opening day, the candidates met with Pennsylvania Governor Lawrence, who apparently decided to commit his Pennsylvania delegates to Kennedy. On Monday, Lawrence met the other presidential aspirants. At this meeting, Senator Symington promised to conduct a vigorous campaign against Nixon; Lyndon B. Johnson emphasized the need for "experienced leadership; while Senator Mike Monroney, in an eloquent plea, proposed a Stevenson-Kennedy ticket. Although Lawrence was impressed with Monroney, he knew that Stevenson couldn't be nominated. John Kennedy spoke about the loss of American prestige abroad and wondered why the people in the underdeveloped countries, who had formerly admired Jefferson, Lincoln and Franklin D. Roosevelt were now quoting excerpts from Karl Marx. As a result, 64 of Pennsylvania's 81 delegates decided to vote for Kennedy.

John Kennedy ran to one state caucus after another, talking, imploring and promising to support the policies of each state. He spoke with the delegations to tell them that *Soapy* Williams and Walter Reuther were in his corner. Then he met with the South Carolina delegation, controlled by the archconservative Governor Ernest Hollings, a very close friend of Bobby Kennedy,and spoke to the Florida delegation headed by Senator Smathers, another good friend of Kennedy (Smathers in fact had been an usher at Kennedy's wedding).

On Monday, John met with the Alaska delegation, promising them a new dam. When the Hawaiians asked what he thought of Senator Joe McCarthy, John said that the issue was dead, much to their dissatisfaction.

On Tuesday, before the count was to begin, Bobby met with his staff at the Bilmore Hotel. They checked out each state to get a final tally.

"I want cold facts," he shouted. "There's no point in fooling ourselves. I want to hear only the votes guaranteed on the first ballot."

The battle to win the large uncommitted states was now concentrated on Minnesota and California, with Governor Orville Freeman standing for Kennedy, and Senator Eugene McCarthy favoring Stevenson. Hubert H. Humphrey held on to the 40 votes he controlled in Minnesota and the Dakota. Nothing Bobby did could sway Humphrey, who was busily intriguing with Lyndon Johnson to get Humphrey second place on the Kennedy ticket.

Joseph L. Rauh, Jr., an important activist in Americans for Democratic Action, and Marvin Rosenberg, a New York businessman who had contributed funds for the Minnesotan's primary campaigns, had attempted to convince their man to get aboard the Kennedy train after the defeat in the West Virginia primary. On July 8, they drove to the Los Angeles International Airport to meet Humphrey, but missed him. The two then drove to the Statler-Hilton Hotel. Rauh rapped sharply on the senator's door, but there was no response. Just as he was about to walk away, he overheard Humphrey's laughter from inside. He turned and rapped on the door again. This time the laughter stopped. Seeing the next door slightly ajar, Rauh looked through and saw Pat O'Connor, an associate of Humphrey, and walked into the suite.

"I stopped at the wrong suite," Paul said. But when he tried to walk into the room, O'Connor blocked his way, shoving him out into the hall, slamming the door in his face.

Inside were James Rowe, a Humphrey man who had joined up with Lyndon B. Johnson and was now one of the Texan's leading activists, Mr. Humphrey and Mr. Johnson. The trio were hatching a plan to stop Kennedy, agreeing to put Humphrey on the ticket for Vice President. Rauh, however, did not know that Kennedy would not have Humphrey on his ticket.

While Johnson, Humphrey, Rowe and Governor Tom Connally were busy concocting schemes to stop Kennedy, Joe was phoning key men from his private lair in Marian Davies' mansion. He knew that Governor Brown had lost control over his California delegation, and that the Texan was using Stevenson, without his knowledge, as a stalking horse to break up the Golden State contingent. The Lone Star State's masterminds wanted Stevenson to draw away the votes from Kennedy, thus stopping Kennedy's momentum. Later, as there was a small likelihood that Stevenson would make it, those votes would wind up in the Johnson column. The vote in the Bear State now stood at 30 for Kennedy, 30 for Stevenson, and the remainder for other hopefuls. Joe was contacting Jesse Unruh, the big daddy of the California Democrats, getting him to swing the votes of the delegation towards his son.

Meanwhile the Stevensonites, encouraged by the sizable number of delegate votes, swung into action. Thousands of young mothers, workers and students marched in front of the Sports Arena shouting their preference for Stevenson. Their voices carried right inside the Arena, making a deep impression on the delegates, especially on those from Kansas and Iowa, who, having pledged their votes to Kennedy, now wanted to vote for a favorite son on the first ballot which could have started a stampede for Stevenson on the second ballot. The Illinois politician, however, had not taken an active part in the campaign. Suddenly, aware of the developing situation, Stevenson left his hotel to talk to his admirers. To show his deep appreciation, he quoted from a poem of Robert Frost:

" 'The woods are lovely and deep. But I have promises to keep. And miles to go before I sleep. And miles to go before I sleep.' "

"The woods" were full of Kennedy-committed delegates, and the scene in the Arena was neither "lovely" nor "deep." Aside from making the delegates go to sleep with his introspective speech, Stevenson managed only to arouse Bobby's suspicions that an evil plot was afoot to overturn his brother's applecart.

Becoming angrier by the minute, Bobby was in a purple rage on seeing Stevenson demonstrators infiltrate into the Arena by twos and threes. Allotted 35 tickets, the devotees were able to get more than 1000 tickets from the 750 Club (a fund-raising arm of the Democratic Party which entitled a member who contributed $10,000 to one ticket). The Host committee of the Party gave another 1,000 tickets to the Stevensonites. In all, they got 4,000 pasteboards.

Bobby was certain that his brother had been double-crossed, and vowed to seek revenge against the diffident Adlai Stevenson. His anger was evident even after his brother had won the nomination. Arthur Schlesinger, Jr. advised him to placate the Stevenson people.

"Arthur," Bobby answered, "human nature requires that you allow 48 hours. Adlai has given us a rough time over the last 48 hours. I will do anything you want, but right now I don't want to hear anything about the Stevensonians. You must allow for human nature."

In the background, however, there was a more dangerous opponent: Lyndon B. Johnson. When the Kennedys invited a few state delegations to speak, Johnson seized that opportunity to challenge Kennedy to a debate before his own state group, also suggesting that Kennedy invite the Massachusetts delegation to the meeting.

Although Bobby had no intention of having his brother debate with the tough-minded Texan, he had lost control of the situation, and Johnson just walked right in.

Dozens of TV commentators and newspaper reporters arrived at the ballroom of the Biltmore Hotel, anticipating a brawl. Bobby walked into the ballroom at 2:00 P.M., pretending he did not know what was going on. When newsmen questioned him, he said that he knew nothing about a "so called debate." He also said that the Texan had not followed the proper protocol when he had bear-trapped John Kennedy to debate the issues.

John F. Kennedy arrived at the ballroom at 3:42 P.M. and spoke about the need to stand up and face the grave problems besetting the nation. His speech was purposefully mild. Out to draw blood, Johnson accused Kennedy of absenteeism in the Congress; he also raised the religious issue:

"I think, Jack, we Protestants proved in West Virginia that we'll vote for a Catholic. What we want is some Catholic votes to prove that they'll vote for a Protestant," adding that Kennedy had missed 45 roll calls when the Civil Rights Bill was being voted on, whereas he had attended every session of the Senate, which wasn't true. Johnson had missed dozens of sessions to avoid voting on bills he didn't like.

In a snide tone, he further implied that Kennedy had supported Eisenhower's low price policy for farm products.

"I hope," Johnson continued, "that you will never forget that I have never at any time during my public career embraced any of the policies of Ezra Taft Benson and his farm program."

Johnson behaved like a leading player in Rex Beach's famous novel, *The Spoiler*. He acted as if he were ready to square off with Kennedy. But the urbane John F. Kennedy smiled and said:

"I don't think I will argue because I don't think Senator Johnson and I disagree on the great issue that face us."

Not appeased, Johnson continued to swing his blunderbus in all directions, implying further that Kennedy was a segregationist, as he had been absent when the Senate was voting to combat the Southern filibuster against the 1960 Civil Rights Bill. "Some senators just weren't there when the chips were down," he declared, conveniently forgetting that he had voted the straight segregationist ticket for years until he suddenly discovered he was a liberal.

Kennedy could have easily deflated Johnson's liberal posture and make mincemeat of the claim that Johnson had never missed a congressional or senatorial roll call. When Johnson boasted that he had stood up to McCarthyism, Kennedy could have quoted from Johnson's eulogy: "Joe McCarthy had strength, he had great courage, he had daring... There was a quality about the man which compelled respect, and even liking, from his strongest adversaries..." This reminder could have made the Texan beat a hasty retreat. And as far as his liberalism was concerned, all Kennedy had to do was to recall that in

1959 Johnson had supported the retention of loyalty oaths for students who asked for loans from the government. Among others, Johnson had opposed statehood for Hawaii because he said it was controlled by Communistic labor unions; favored giving Franco of Spain a $100,000,000 loan; and voted for the McCarran Anti-Subversive Bill which was termed a vicious piece of legislation by church spokesmen and civil libertarians.

Johnson presented himself as a hard-working, mature and responsible legislator, a man with grey in his hair. On the other hand, he portrayed Kennedy as the handsome playboy, a dilettante who would ruin the country.

Ignoring Johnson's remarks, and with quiet sarcasm, Kennedy said, "I strongly support him for Majority Leader. You stick to your old job and I'll handle the Presidency."

Johnson left the two-state delegation meeting in a jubilant mood, certain he had scored a victory. But Governor John Connally, who had engineered the confrontation, knew better. Johnson had behaved like a typical arm-flaying frontier-type politician. Kennedy, on the other hand, had impressed those who were at the meeting as a self-possessed, sophisticated politician who had exercised a great deal of self-control.

With typical Texan exaggeration, Johnson bragged to newsmen that he was plucking off Kennedy's delegates like over-ripe grapes off a vine. "California," he boasted, "was turning into a real setback. Indiana was restive. New Mexico had shown that Kennedy support is mythical, and so was Minnesota. Iowa refused to go over. Look at Daleware. The Canal Zone went for me. Kansas refused to flop. Ohio and Maryland don't want to be hogtied. They want to rise and express themselves."

But it was all a pipe dream. While he was giving his version of the race for the nomination, Kennedy racked up an additional 30 delegates from New Jersey.

On learning what was happening, Governor Connally started a smear campaign against Kennedy. Mrs. India Edwards, former Chairwoman of the National Democratic organization and an ally of Connally, reported that Kennedy would not be alive if it were not for cortizone: "Kennedy had a mild form of Addison's disease."

On July 4, just as the delegates were about to vote for their candidate, Johnson commented: "I wasn't any Chamberlain-umbrella policy man. I never thought that Hitler was right," he said, referring to Joe Sr.'s isolationist views during World War II. "When Joe McCarthy was on the march and someone had to stand up and be counted, I was voting liberal. Every Democratic senator stood up and voted with the leader."

Senator Eugene McCarthy of Minnesota, on the other hand, delivered an impassioned speech extolling the manifold virtues of Adlai Stevenson.

"Do not reject this man," he pleaded. "Do not leave this prophet without honor in his own party."

Four thousand Stevensonites in the gallery together with the multitude outside roared their approval. Pandemonium broke out on the convention floor. But despite the well-organized demonstration, the big city bosses stood firm for Kennedy. They had no intentions of picking another William Jennings Bryan to lead them into the political wilderness. Stevenson knew that he would not make it. He learned to his chagrin that the big city bosses had long since committed themselves to Kennedy, and that although Eleanor Roosevelt, Herbert Lehman and Finlettes were still supporting him, they were preoccupied with their fight against Carmine DeSapio, the chieftain of Tammany Hall.

A few months before the national convention, Bobby, in a rather indelicate manner, said to the New York reform leaders, "Gentlemen, I don't give a damn if the State and County organizations survive after November. I want to elect John F. Kennedy." And later he told DeSapio that "the only thing I am interested in is electing Senator Kennedy, President."

Stevenson, who certainly was not a neophite in politics, should have known that Joe Sr. and Bobby had had the nomination sewed up.

By Wednesday morning, Bobby was certain that the nomination was in the bag with a total of 739 plus votes. A liason man, who had stayed close to the New Jersey delegation, phoned Bobby to tell him that Governor Meyner was still holding on to his 41 votes. Bobby promised that Meyner would never get a job with the Kennedy Administration unless he released them to his brother.

With the balloting about to begin, John Kennedy moved to a hideaway apartment on North Rossmore Boulevard to watch the process on television. On discovering the set wasn't working, he ran downstairs and knocked on the door of actor William Gargan, who, clad in pajamas, invited Kennedy to enter.

Meanwhile, at the Marian Davies mansion, Joe stopped phoning the delegates to sit down to watch the balloting.

Bobby, on the other hand, in a calm mood, watched the balloting in the control-point cottage near the Arena. Before it begun, John phoned Bobby to check the delegate vote, and found their tallies agreeing.

Alabama was the first: 20 votes for Lyndon B. Johnson, three for Kennedy. Then the rest continued with monotonous regularity, with Kennedy getting most of the states. By the time it came to Wyoming, Kennedy had 748 votes — not enough. When McCraken, the state's national committeeman, sang out:

"Wyoming casts all 15 votes for the next President of the United States." Kennedy went over the top by two votes—final results: 806 for Kennedy, 409 for Johnson.

When the vote was announced, Bobby and Pierre Salinger jumped to their feet, hugging everyone in sight, and prancing around to cottage. The Texans, on the other hand, were bitter. They had just suffered another *Alamo.* "Okay, okay, okay," they moaned. "They can have their Kennedy. But we'll be back here in four years to nominate Lyndon."

After the balloting was completed, the party leaders left the convention hall and made a beeline towards the cottage. Among those who came to pay homage were John Bailey, Mike DeSalle, Richard Daley, Governor David L. Lawrence, Congressman William Green, Averill Harriman, Mike Prendegast, G. Memnen Williams, Abraham Ribicoff, and many others.

John F. Kennedy walked in a few minutes later with the power elite of the Democratic Party deferring to him, stepping forward to shake his hand, one at a time. Outside the lesser fry stood waiting patiently.

After delivering a brief acceptance speech, he left for a much needed rest in his North Rossmore rooms where he had two scrambled eggs, toast, jelly and two glasses of milk before going to bed.

Chapter 11

The Choice of a Vice-Presidential Candidate

It was a bone-tired man who left the Sports Arena on Thursday, July 14 at 2 A.M. to find some sercease from the nerve-wracking tension at his temporary home on North Rossmore Boulevard. Kennedy's staff was under the impression that the second place would go to either Senator Henry M. *Scoop* Jackson or to Senator Stuart Symington of Missouri. A rumor had Governor Orville Freeman of Minnesota a first choice.

No one suspected that Lyndon B. Johnson was being considered for second place. John had admitted he enterntained a deep admiration for the Texan whom he thought qualified to be the party's candidate.

Johnson had said things about Kennedy that should never have been mentioned. Despite those outward appearances, Kennedy told Philip Graham, publisher of the *Washington Post,* that Johnson would probably accept an offer to run for Vice-President.

A few weeks earlier, Hal Boggs, a Louisiana Democrat, had made a bet that the ticket would be Kennedy and Johnson. Boggs, a close friend of both, was in a position to know what was on their minds. Bobby Baker had a chat with Theodore Sorensen, saying that the ticket would include Johnson. Although Sorensen expressed doubt that Johnson would settle for second place, Baker was sure it would happen that way.

Kennedy prided himself on being a pragmatist, knowing that the election could be lost if the Southern states voted Republican. The Dixie electoral total was of prime importance and only Johnson was in a position to deliver them.

When Graham first mentioned the idea, Johnson let loose with a stream of colorful invectives that shocked the polished publisher into a stunned silence.

On leaving the cottage to go to his temporary sleeping quarters, John first phoned his father to tell him that he was thinking of picking Johnson. Joe thought it was a smart move, saying that the liberals would probably stage a revolt but had nowhere to go. "The step," he said, "would look good in a couple of weeks from now." Bobby, on the other hand, did not like Johnson and was plugging for his friend Senator Henry Jackson with whom he had been intimate friends since the two served on the Senate Select Committee. Meanwhile, Speaker Sam Rayburn was having a telephone conversation with Johnson, advising him not to accept it. Johnson, however, promised Rayburn that he would not make a final decision before he had consulted him. By evening, Joe called Johnson to induce him to accept his son's offer. Johnson replied that he had not planned to relinquish his post as Majority Leader. Joe reiterated that a Vice President exercises more power than a mere Majority Leader.

At about 7:30 A.M., John Kennedy went to the Biltmore Hotel headquarters. At 8:00, he telephoned Johnson, who said he would be happy to discuss the possibility. Before he went to see Kennedy, however, Johnson phoned Rayburn.

Kennedy walked into the Johnson suite and told the Texan of his desire to have him on the ticket as he "was best qualified by experience" but as a political realist, he must know that "as a Southerner it would [have been] impossible to have him nominated for first place." John also reminded Johnson that he had said on many occasions that the country would be in good hands if Johnson were to take over should anything happen to him.

Johnson played hard to convince. He told Kennedy that he would still prefer to remain the Majority Leader in the Senate and in any event he had promised to discuss it with Sam Rayburn, with Governor Price Daniels, and with his wife before deciding.

When John returned to his suite, he phoned Bobby and asked him to check on the number of electoral votes controlled by the Northern tier and Texas. Shortly after 9:00 A.M., Pierre Salinger and Kenneth O'Donnell went to see Bobby, who was taking a bath.

"Get me the book and find how many delegates there are in the North plus Texas," he asked Salinger.

The usually ebullient Salinger suddenly assumed a grave air.

"You're not thinking of that?"

"Yes, we are," Bobby replied.

John held court in Suite 9333 of the Biltmore where party leaders learned that Johnson had been picked for second place. Governor David Lawrence was first to enter, then Robert F. Wagner of New York, Harriman, DeSapio, Mike Prendegast,

DeSalle, John Bailey, Ribicoff and a host of others, most taking the Kennedy choice in good grace. It did not go down well with the union leaders and such Northern liberals as Alex Rose, David Dubinsky, and Walter Reuther of the U.A.W., who violently opposed the choice. Some warned that the Negroes would never vote for the Texan, and Kennedy couldn't convince them. On leaving the room, they went to sulk in Reuther's suite.

The inner-Kennedy circle of O'Donnell, O'Brien and Powers gathered in Kennedy's suite to receive the official word that Johnson was the chosen one. O'Donnell, who had tried to get the nomination for Symington, told Kennedy that the Americans for Democratic Action would never go along with that choice. In an irritable mood, John told O'Donnell that he did not want any back talk.

Jackson and Symington, who were under the illusion that they were the prime choice, were waiting for the word in their respective suites. Rumors were flying all over the hotel: Jackson was told that he was the man; a minute later, Symington heard that he had been picked. Hopes soared up and down, like a *watered* stock on the day before a big market break. Big Jim Farley thought that Symington was the best man for the job. On being told that Johnson would be picked, he said that it was "impossible".

Senator Jackson was told that Johnson had been chosen, to his disappointment. In his press conference of 3:00 P.M., in an almost inaudible voice, he said: "At about 3:00 this afternoon Senator Kennedy called me over and advised me after careful and thoughtful consideration he had decided that Senator Johnson should be the Democratic Vice-President nominee."

When James Blair of the Missouri delegation heard that, he turned to Senator Symington: "Partner, we've been run over by a steamroller."

Arthur Schlesinger moaned: "I'm sick.

While the liberals were in an uproar, Rayburn told Johnson to accept. It was none other than the very busy Hale Boggs (later to die in a plane crash), a confidant of both men who had convinced Rayburn to change his mind. When Johnson asked Rayburn what had changed his mind, he said: "I'm a damn sight smarter this morning than I was last night." But the real reason was the fear that Nixon instead might occupy the White House.

The very colorful but ruthless Senator Robert Kerr of Oklahoma, who had amassed a huge fortune in oil, told Johnson that he would be in hot water if he accepted Kennedy's invitation.

"If you take Kennedy's offer," he threatened, "I'm going to

get my 30-30 and shoot you between the eyes."

In the labor camp, David MacDonald, the leader of the Steel Workers Union, was the only big labor boss who approved. Alex Rose, President of the Hat and Millinary Union, continued to voice his distaste of the Texan, warning that the ticket would never be accepted by his organization's rank and file, and Walter Reuther was "not enthusiastic."

Worried and afraid that the entire Michigan delegation would abandon the ticket, Bobby went to see Williams at his suite:

"*Jack* wants Lyndon."

Thanks to Bobby, the liberal revolt began to fizzle. He was running all over the hotel, talking with delegates, asking them for their support. He even had the task to tell Johnson to bow out gracefully should the liberals refuse to go along. Furthermore, the Michigan delegation found Johnson unpalatable. When Bobby proposed the national chairmanship of the party, Johnson was perturbed, "The *boy* is trying to kick me off the ticket," he said with a certain inflection. Then he went on with numerous expressions. When Rayburn walked into the room and learned what Bobby was up to, Johnson let loose another stream of invectives. Although Bobby was really innocent, Johnson never believed it.

"My job," Bobby said, "was to act as a middle man. I had also been instructed by my brother to let Johnson know that it [the nomination] was not to be unanimous. That my brother felt an obligation to convey to him the likelihood of a floor flight so that Johnson would have the option of refusing if he wished to avoid embarrassment. I was to say who was opposed to him and why, and to say my brother would understand if he wanted to back out; and if this were the case my brother wanted to offer him the chairmanship of the Democratic National Committee so that he would have an effective and controlling voice in the campaign."

The extremely sensitive Johnson told Bobby that he had never expected unanimity, but that he did want to deal directly with the candidate himself.

Philip Graham, who had been listening, decided to go to Kennedy's headquarters, suspicious that someone was trying to convince Kennedy to dump Johnson. As he was about to leave, Ladybird Johnson told him that she did not want her husband to take the job. After several minutes of added confusion because of telephone mix-ups and malfunctions, John got through to Johnson:

"I want you to take it," John said matter of factly.

57

Johnson, sitting on his bed, listened to the draft statement, finally convinced that he was going to be on the ticket.

John then spoke to the labor leaders and their liberal allies to reassure them. Bobby piped in and said:

"Johnson would add a great deal in certain sections because of his excellent reputation and for the many things he has contributed to the Senate and to the country."

Bobby had obviously forgotten he had attempted to have Senator Jackson for second place, having raised objections over Johnson. Williams and the delegation from the District of Columbia were still not convinced about Johnson. A floor fight quickly ensued.

While the battle was in progress, Johnson telephoned former Vice President Garner in Texas, to tell him about the Vice Presidency. The grizzled old farmer retorted that the job was not worth "a bucket of warm spit." But Johnson now thought otherwise, even though he felt a deep resentment against Bobby.

Johnson really believed that Bobby was working to keep him off the ticket. As a result, that feeling was to mar their relations for years to come.

The whole thing started when Bobby walked into the Johnson suite along with Larry O'Brien and Kenneth O'Donnel to soothe those delegates who objected to Johnson as a candidate for the Vice Presidency.

Charles Bartlett, a close friend of Kennedy and a syndicated columnist, reported that Bobby wanted Symington as his second man. A few of his advisors, all artful dogers, had suggested that he first offer the nomination to Johnson. According to Bartlett, Kennedy was profoundly shocked when Jackson agreed to accept the offer, because he had been assured by his advisors that Johnson would not have accepted.

Bobby later described the incident in this way: "I think it was also taken for granted by virtually everyone that if he [Johnson] were interested he would be the choice. My brother thought highly of Johnson's ability, but it seemed inconceivable to any of us that he would accept. Someone suggested that he might be interested and the possibility explored. My brother decided to do so, especially after talking with my father. Our role was that of agent. It was unimportant whether or not I concurred in the opinion. My brother was definitely happy to have him on the ticket. That was enough for us."

Chapter 12

The Campaign

The victorious but harassed John Kennedy could hardly speak, his voice practically gone. Needing rest, he went to his summer home in Hyannis Port along with Bobby, their political henchmen and close friends. A few days later, John met with his staff on Bobby's green lawn. The men sat on eight green chaise lounges inter-connected with green telephone cords.

Others participating were Kenneth O'Donnel, Lawrence O'Brien, Stephen Smith, cigar-smoking Pierre Salinger, John Baily, and Jim Rowe— often referred to as the *Irish Mafia.*

Now a seasoned campaigner, Bobby, recalling the time when he was on the Stevenson staff, said: "Nobody asked me anything, nobody wanted me to do anything, nobody consulted me so I had time to watch everything. I filled notebooks with notes on how a Presidential campaign should be run."

The youngest campaign manager in the history of the nation had one definite advantage over his competitors: he was the brother of the candidate with whom he shared reciprocal, deep and loyal feelings. In his new role, he had to reconcile the differences and to control his gruff way of speaking to others.

The New York State Democratic organization was in a mess over the fight between Carmine DeSapio, Mike Prendegast and the Tammany boys. Although Bobby was able to resolve the problem, he did not succeed in controlling his gruffness. As a result, he aroused a great deal of bad feeling.

His manner simply did not impress individuals like Herbert Lehman. To make things worse, he appeared on a Barry Gray radio show wherein he criticised Harry Byrd of Virginia and Congressman Howard Smith of the House Rules committee, accusing them of blocking important bills. That wasn't all: he tackled Jackie Robinson, the former baseball star and the director of personnel for the Chock Full O'Nuts, insinuating that the FBI had gathered unsavory facts on him. During a heated discussion, he produced a dossier containing red-hot items about Robinson's boss, Mr. Black, which proved that the head of the restaurant chain was a "great booster of Nixon." The even-tempered Robinson did not mince words: "If the younger Kennedy is going to resort to lies, then I can see what kind of campaign this is going to be... Apparently, young Bobby hasn't heard that the Emancipation Proclamation was signed 97 years ago. He doesn't run any plantation and I suggest to Kennedy that he stop acting as if he did."

The brawl on the Barry Gray program presented a serious problem for John Kennedy. With the Southern politicians in an uproar, he promised he would control his brother Bobby, admitting that his brother's remarks were most "unfortunate," attributing Bobby's behavior to fast-burn reactions.

Bobby, however, was much too busy to waste his time dwelling on past tactical blunders. His job was to influence the delegates from New York, Pennsylvania, California, Michigan, Texas, Illinois, Ohio, New Jersey and Massachusetts— states representing 237 out of 269 electoral votes needed to win. Bobby, therefore, had to get an additional 60 or 70 votes from Dixieland, the New England or the Midwestern states. To insure victory, it was decided to let Johnson assume the responsibility for the Dixieland states including Texas.

Congressman Frank *Toppel* Thompson was placed in charge of voter registration to lure the more than 40,000,000 unregistered Americans.

The National Committee was established in Washington. From those offices, Bobby and Larry O'Brien coordinated the local *Pros* and the volunteers, with Bobby insuring that men from Michigan be assigned to work in California, and those from New York to work in Rhode Island, for in his eyes, outsiders could judge problems more objectively. His staff at times ran over 200 men and women. Coordinating them required intelligence, and a lot of patience— something Bobby still lacked. Berating them was not unusual.

"What are you doing!" Bobby yelled at Theodore White. "Let's get on the road tomorrow. I want us all to be on the road tomorrow. I want us all to be on the road."

There were many honest men and women who were deeply concerned about having a Roman Catholic in the White House. They thought that a man of that faith would not be able to be objective on questions concerning the separation of church and state. The issue took on an ugly turn when the Reverend Norman Vincent Peale and a group of prominent Protestant clergymen met in Washington. The churchmen questioned the sincerity of a Catholic candidate regarding his loyalty to the dictates of the cardinals and bishops of his church. Newspaper reaction to Peale's declaration was decidedly unfavorable. Small wonder! Peale and his fellow clergymen had said that a Chief Executive who happened to be Roman Catholic would find himself "under extreme pressure by the hierarchy of his church" to adhere to the "commands of the Vatican." They thought that the religious issue was the "most significant one" and they also believed that Kennedy would feel himself to be "duty-bound to admit its direction."

Kennedy was given an opportunity to refute that contention at the Greater Houston Ministerial Association: "I believe in an America where the separation of church and state is absolute— where no Catholic prelate would tell the President how to act, and no Protestant minister would tell his parishioners for whom to vote, where no church or church-school is granted any funds or political preferences."

On being asked why he had refused to come to the consecration of an interfaith chapel in Philadelphia, erected to commemorate the death of the four chaplains killed by a torpedo from a German submarine, he explained that he had been invited neither as a layman nor as a congressman, but as a representative of a religious faith, assuring his audience that he would have gone if the invitation had been worded differently. Another asked whether he would permit his church to dictate actions to the President. Again he reassured he would not permit them to influence him in any way.

About a month later, Bobby brought up the religious issue in Indiana. Clinton Green, an old Democratic Party warhorse, was asked to persuade Bobby not to raise the religious issue in any of his speeches. The state had been a stronghold of the Ku Klux Klan during the 1920's, which, though no longer powerful, still had a strong anti-Catholic sentiment.

Mathan Walsh, who was running for governor, was a member of the Christian Church while his wife and children were Catholics. Green told Bobby that Walsh was underplaying the religious issue as he was afraid that the Republicans would point to the fact that the wife and children were Catholics. Bobby, therefore, would only aggravate the problem by bringing up his brother's religious faith. Without saying anything to Green, Bobby mentioned John Kennedy's religious affiliations in every speech he made, telling his listeners that Al Smith had been defeated because he was Catholic, that some people thought that Catholics were simple bodies walking around with horns on their heads, but that Catholics had made many sacrifices for their country in World Wars I and II— that his older brother Joe had lost his life in War, reminding the Hossiers that John Kennedy had been injured in action while commanding his PT-109. "The Catholics," he emphasized, "have performed major services for their country."

He praised Konrad Adenauer and General Charles DeGaulle and said that both men were Catholics: "Would [you] have voted against these two men just because they were Catholics?"

Clinton Green, who toured the state with Bobby, said that the Kennedys "were the ones who brought up the religious issue and kept it alive. It wasn't the Republicans."

The Kennedys had first used the issue in 1956 when they were trying to get Johnson as Stevenson's running mate. The *Baily Report,* which had been compiled by Ted Sorensen, and now released by the Kennedys, stressed that most of the important industrial states had large Catholic populations of vital importance in any election; it also stated that the Protestant voters lived in the smaller states, asserting that Kennedy, as a consequence, would be able to win most of the Catholic votes.

Stewart Alsop, a Kennedy friend, wrote in the *Saturday Evening Post* that "Kennedy's Catholicism is a vitally important factor in his campaign, partly because there is no great domestic issue between the two parties to smother and override the religious issue."

The Catholic issue which Bobby emphasized was one of the basic gimmicks worked out long before the 1960 campaign. Raising the issue was more than justified from a political point of view. It served to bring prosperous Catholics back into the Democratic camp; at the same time, it convinced Protestants to vote for a Catholic.

The liberal Catholic publication Commonwheal criticized Bobby: "Candidates, who by devious means accent their religious affiliations where it helps and play them down where it may be handicap, are cheating." But no one paid any attention to it.

During their Florida stop-over, Dr. Martin Luther King, Jr. and 52 civil rights workers staged a sitdown in the Magnolia Room, a restaurant located in the Rich Department Store in Atlanta, resulting in the arrest of Dr. King and a sentence of four months at hard labor. In tears, and afraid that her husband might be killed, Mrs. Coretta King talked with Justice Department officials.

Bobby and John Kennedy had been warned that if they interfered too much in the politics of the deep South, they could lose the election. Bobby's first reaction was not to interfere, afraid that a pro-King stand would swing Southern whites into the camp of Kennedy's Republican opponent Richard M. Nixon.

Professor Harris Wofford of Notre Dame University, and a staff member of Sargent Shriver's Civil Rights Section, together with another colleague, proposed that Kennedy should come to the assistance of Dr. King. Wofford contacted Shriver, who got in touch with John, who immediately called Mrs. King to assure her that he would do all he could to save her husband. He then told Bobby to have Dr. King released. Although he got mad as hell, Bobby phoned the judge, asking for King's release. Bobby's staff prepared and distributed two million pieces of literature giving pertinent facts about the Georgia incident.

After it was over, Bobby said, "You bomb throwers better not do anything more in this campaign." He was referring to Shriver and Wofford.

When Columnist Murray Kempton asked if he was glad he put through the call to Georgia, Bobby said, "Sure I'm glad but I would hope I'm not glad for the reason you think I'm glad."

In Chicago alone, over 250,000 blacks voted for Kennedy. In other big cities, Kennedy received overwhelming numbers.

In Texas, Kennedy won by a meager 45,000 votes, thanks to the Negro vote which also won South Carolina.

The Republican National Committee made special study of the Negro vote in Philadelphia and found that Kennedy had received 82% and Nixon 18% of the votes.

Bobby was in a nervous state as the campaign reached its climax, and his temper correspondingly short. When a member of his staff told him that things were going well in upstate New York, he snarled, "You know damned well they are not going pretty good."

He brushed off Frank Sinatra and Walter Reuther, telling both not to become active in the campaign, as they could do "more harm than good." He was also annoyed with Johnson's habit of cancelling out on his speaking engagements at the last moment. He saw red when Johnson failed to go to Honolulu as planned, necessitating appeasing many local Democrats. Worse was the fact that Bobby could do nothing to control Johnson, who went on his merry way rescheduling his speaking tour as he pleased.

John Kennedy returned to Boston a day before the election, with a grand tour of the city. Old-line Irish politicians, some looking like comedians with their ruddy complexions and red noses, gathered at the Sports Garden to hear him speak. Afterwards, he went to the historic Faneuil Hall for a televised speech; finally to the Statler Hotel for a few hours rest. And Bobby, who had worked harder than any member of his staff, was almost drunk with fatigue.

Next morning, at 8:43 A.M., John and Jackie went to vote at the long-abandoned West End branch of the Boston Public Library, his voting address still listed as 122 Bowdoin Street. Soon after, they flew to Hyannis Port to join Bobby, Ethel, Teddy and Joan, Pat and Peter Lawford, Eunice, Sargent Shriver, Stephen Smith and his wife Jean.

John tried to relax in his cottage, but was too restless. He walked outside and watched Bobby playing touch football with Eunice. Then he went inside, with Caroline walking by his side.

The election returns began to come in late afternoon from areas of Maine, Tennessee, Alabama and other Eastern states, showing Nixon ahead. By 7:00 P.M., the big city results began to roll in, making it increasingly evident that Kennedy was capturing the big cities. By midnight, Kennedy was ahead by 2,000,000. Pollster Louis Harris gave Nixon a 60-40 edge for the farm and border states where Kennedy was trailing.

The election headquarters had been established at Bobby's house, with telephone exchanges replacing other furniture. Fourteen girls manned the phones which were connected to the Democratic headquarters and to other states. Two lines linked the headquarters with dozens of poll watchers. Another two were reserved for special messages from important local leaders.

Because the votes were not coming in large volume, Bobby became worried. He phoned Sid Woolner in Michigan, who gave no encouragement. Then he called Richard Daley in Chicago, who assured him that all would come out well in the end. Bobby called Jesse Unruh in California, who was pessimistic about Kennedy's chances in that state.

Exhausted, John went to bed at 4:40 A.M. While sleeping, the Michigan vote came in turning the tide in his favor, and thus the Presidency.

In large measure, Bobby had been responsible for his brother winning the election. When asked what had pleased him most in life, Bobby said, "The most important of all was the Presidential campaign of 1960."

Chapter 13

After the Election

In a speech at the Alfalfa Club in Washington, D.C., the President said that to be a good Attorney General, one would need sound judgment, a willingness to work, and an ability to learn. Since his brother Bobby had all those qualities, he had decided to appoint him as the chief law officer of the nation.

In a humorous aside, he asked his audience what was wrong with a fellow getting a little legal training before going into the practice of law. Although it brought down the house, Bobby did not appreciate it, later mentioning it to the President, who replied that a man in public life should be able to take "kidding" in stride. But, Bobby retorted: "You were reaching for a laugh at my expense."

Bobby's reaction was not surprising. Arthur Krock, the *New York Times* columnist, and an old friend of the Kennedy family, once wrote that Bobby "is a very different personality. There is not the gentleness or the sweetness there was in his brother. His brother had not only these, but more. Bobby Kennedy has a good sense of humor and he has wit, but he hasn't got the objective sense of humor that John F. Kennedy had. *Jack* could find himself rather absurd and ridiculous at times. Bobby never, never, could. Bobby can feel chagrined at having made a mistake; can laugh at a joke based on that, but he does not really enjoy it."

Bobby never relished taking on the job as Attorney General, preferring one at the sub-Cabinet level in the Defense or State Departments. But John insisted that only the Justice Department was right, for the new Secretary of State would not like the idea of having the President's younger brother breathing down his back.

Joe had a good deal to say about the subject. He even told his friends he couldn't understand why Bobby was so reluctant about taking the job. He urged Bobby to take it, assuring him that he would be the best Attorney General since Harlan Fiske

Stone, the brilliant legal mind who later became Chief Justice of the Supreme Court.

Malicious people said that Joe Sr. wanted to staff the upper echelons of the government with "his people," surmising that Teddy would be the Majority leader of the Senate, Bobby would run the State Department, taking over John's Presidency after the two terms, and in the years to come, Joe Sr.'s grandchildren would solidify the dynasty by consolidating positions within the three branches of the government.

Bobby kept on playing the role of a reluctant dragon. To avoid a confrontation with John, who would not take no for an answer, Bobby decided to take a vacation in Europe with his family. Joe Sr. couldn't believe what was happening: "I don't know what's wrong with him. *Jack* needs all the good men he can get. There is no one better than Bobby."

Intimate friends suggested that Bobby take the Senate seat vacated by John, but he retorted:

"I won't take it. The only way I'll go to the Senate is to run for it."

With the Cabinet completed, Bobby, still confused, went to see J. Edgar Hoover for advice. Among other things, he asked whether he should take the job, if there was more work to be done in the war against crime, if he could be of any value at the Justice Department, etc. Then he went to talk with William Rogers, the Attorney General about to retire. Then he phoned his brother to tell him that he still hadn't decided to accept the appointment. The next morning, Bobby went to have breakfast with John at 3307 N Street in Georgetown.

After conferring upstairs for a few minutes, they walked downstairs where they were joined by John Siegenthalar. The President told Bobby to stop procrastinating and to take the position, appealing to his sense of duty and responsibility, saying that Dean Rusk and C. Douglas Dillon had accepted government jobs at considerable financial sacrifice, further pointing out that Adlai Stevenson had agreed to become the U.S. Ambassador to the United Nations, and reminding Bobby that all of the Cabinet appointees, with the sole exception of Governor Ribicoff, were complete strangers— men who had placed duty to the nation above all personal considerations.

"How can you refuse?... We'll announce it at midnight so no one will notice it," the President remarked with an obvious smile.

Outside, newspapermen crowded the street. As the President and Bobby were about to leave, Bobby's hair became rather disheveled due to the wind.

"Dammit, Bobby, comb your hair," the President said.

It was obvious that Bobby's appointment did not meet with the unanimous approval of many editorial writers. The editors of *The New York Times* expressed negative comments about Bobby's "lack of experience."

Professor Bickle, in the *New Republic*— a publication well-disposed towards Kennedy— recalled Bobby's record as the Chief counsel for the McClellan Committee:

"Mr. Kennedy appears to find congenial the role of prosecutor, judge and jury, all consolidated in his one efficient person...

"No doubt he sought to serve the public interest as he saw it. And the answer on the record is that he has tunnel vision; he sees the public interest in terms of ends with little appreciation of the significance of means... The meaning of due process, of the adversary process of accusation and defense before judges disinterested in the immediate outcome, is that the government suffers itself to concede it possible that it may be wrong. Mr. Kennedy's assured righteousness is in vivid contrast..."

The Attorney General is the nation's chief executive law officer; he (or she) is required to regard the means above ends and the process above results. He exercises the only civilian control over the FBI whose files contain vast amounts of unprocessed "knowledge," presiding as judge, very often as a court of last resort over a myriad deportation cases, and choosing whom to prosecute and when.

"His ultimate abuse of the congressional investigating procedure," Bickle had pointed out, was "the notion that a Plea of the Fifth Amendment is the same as an admission of guilt. It isn't yet. No one since McCarthy has done more than Mr. Kennedy to foster the impression that the plea is the same as a confession of guilt."

Professor Bickle further said that society's cumbersome method of getting at the truth did not concern Bobby too much.

The *Olympian* Walter Lippmann couldn't make up his mind about the appointment. "There are some who say that he has not yet acquired a sufficiently highly refined and mellow sense of due process."

Gravel-voiced Senator Everett McKinley Dirksen had doubts about a man who had never had any courtroom experience. Senator Gordon Allot, Republican from Colorado, could not "in good conscience vote to sustain the nomination of a man who was less qualified than thousands of other lawyers in the nation to be the Attorney General."

Despite all those misgivings, Bobby was confirmed. John F.

Kennedy was certain that Bobby would prove to be an asset, a feeling shared by Jackie as well.

In a copy of his book, *The Enemy Within*, (bound in red leather by a London bookmaker, two months after her husband had become President), on the first page Jackie wrote: "To Bobby, who made the impossible and changed all of our lives. With love, Jackie."

Several close friends also questioned the advisability of Bobby's appointment. He was too young, one said; others did not like his attitude towards civil liberties; to another, Bobby was too vindictive to be trusted with such awesome powers, and Joe's remark that Bobby was a "good hater"— just like him, didn't help. Yet, no one saw the compulsiveness in Bobby's character— a trait, perhaps more than any other, that may have been a cause for his successes, and, his eventual demise.

Why had the President insisted in having his brother as his Attorney General when Bobby really didn't want the position? The fact is that the President needed a man whom he could trust, an official who was willing to take the rap for unpopular decisions. Bobby, the loyal brother, was the only one ready to assume the pose of the man tough enough to say *no* in public.

One of the major problems of the new Administration was the civil rights question. Blacks were no longer content to accept counterfeit coins, having waited since 1954, the year of the Supreme Court decision to get the government moving on intergrating the schools in the North and the South. The President knew he had to move cautiously; he had won the election by only 100,000 votes, far too small to make him feel that he had received a genuine mandate from the people. His problem was how to maintain good relations with the Southern Democrats and keep the blacks in a good frame of mind at the same time.

In a speech before Kennedy's Inaugural, Dr. Martin Luther King said that " the Negro vote elected the President and we must not hesitate to remind him of that," a sentiment shared by many other black leaders.

Many of Bobby's close associates thought he would be to shy to tell off the segregationists. They were wrong. Bobby could berate men twice his age. Richard Rovere, the political writer, was told that Bobby "is quite capable of telling Governor Ribicoff to stay after school and order John Kenneth Galbraith to write 'Procrastination is the thief of time' 500 times."

Among other things, Bobby was instrumental in naming Robert McNamara Secretary of Defense.

When the President proposed Douglas Dillon for the Treasury post, Bobby raised doubts about the advisability of having a Wall Street Republican in charge of fiscal policies. He wanted to know if Dillon were to resign, would he issue a sharp critique against the financial policies of the government? Should the Administration be a captive of a Republican? The President agreed to have Bobby question Dillon. In his usual blunt fashion, Bobby asked him what he would do under such circumstances. A little astonished, Dillon assured that if he were to resign, he would leave quietly.

Bobby was out to find the best men for the various posts in the Administration. He chose Byron White, the former All-American football player, as his deputy Attorney General, asking him to come up with a tough lawyer to enforce the civil rights enactments. He would have to be under no circumstances "a professional civil righter," otherwise the Southern legislators would not confirm him. White asked Harris Wofford for suggestions and in turn he recommended Burke Marshall, a Yale University classmate. Bobby, who had never heard of Marshall, had him investigated and found him as clean as the proverbial hound's tooth.

The Southerners, however, weren't buying a pig in a poke. Senator Owin Johnson wanted to know why Marshall had joined the American Civil Liberties Union, and Senator Eastland wanted to know if Marshall planned to solicit complaints.

"In what field do you mean?" Marshall asked.

"Voting rights."

"No, the Department does not solicit complaints in any field. I expect, however, that we might as the Division in the past makes record demands where there has not been a complaint."

"Where you have no aggrieved parties who made complaints, you would bring suits anyway? Is that what you say?" Senator Eastland asked.

Marshall told the legislator that he would not file suits in cases where he did not believe anything could be proved, but that they would definitely be filed in cases which could stand up in court even before a complaint would have been registered.

"What criteria would you use in selecting the area?" Senator Eastland asked.

"I think one important criteria would be the statistics on registration and voting. If the statistics on registration and voting in particular cases showed a heavy imbalance against race, I think that we would consider that to be sufficient to start an investigation."

Chairman Eastland wanted to know if Marshall planned to look into the voting records in other areas of the country. Marshall blandly replied that he had not seen "any evidence of discrimination on account of race which would warrant the records demand outside the South."

This new staff member was telling the powerful Senator that he was going into his home state of Mississippi and other areas of Dixie to wage a battle for Negro rights there.

Senator Eastland and his colleagues intended to filibuster Marshall's confirmation. Unbeknownst to them, Marshall was already working at the Justice Department. Bobby, who was growing very impatient with Eastland's sabotaging the confirmation, had no intention of playing games with the Southerner. Unexpectedly, Bobby walked into the Senate room where the hearing was being conducted, sat down, and with his piercing blue eyes glowered at the Senator, looking like an avenging angel. Intimidated, both Eastland and the other Senators quickly voted to confirm Marshall.

Bobby's predecessor, William Rogers, had always handled Eastland with kid gloves, receiving a great deal of cooperation especially because Roger never pressed on the civil rights issue.

With Bobby, things were going to be different: "I have the impression that people in the Department of Justice wanted to do more [on civil rights] but were held back by a general hands-off policy in the past administration. This won't be true in the future."

Bobby was committed to enforce the decision of the Supreme Court. But although most people believed what he said, black leaders questioned the extent of his emotional commitment, and invited him to meet with them.

Present were writer James Baldwin; Lorraine Hansbery, the playwrite; Jerome Smith, the Negro leader who had been severely beaten by a mob of Southern racists; Harry Bellafonte and Professor Clark of City College. Smith opened by saying that he felt like vomiting for being in the same room with the Attorney General. Bobby took the remark as a personal insult, retorting in kind. Smith rejoined that as long as Negroes were treated like animals, he felt no moral obligation to fight for the United States in a war— to the applause of the group. Baldwin added that white troops had been sent to Alabama because a white man had been stabbed. Burke Marshall answered that he had consulted Dr. King before ordering the troops, causing hysterical laughter. When Bobby presented his thoughts, they showed no interest. According to Bobby, Baldwin wasn't even aware that the President had given a civil rights message to the Congress in February.

"They didn't know anything," he said. "They don't know

what the laws are. They don't know what the facts are. They
don't know what we've been doing or what we've been trying to
do. You couldn't talk to them as you can to Roy Wilkins or
Martin Luther King. They didn't want to talk to us. It was all
emotion and hysteria. They stood up and orated. They cursed.
Some of them wept and walked out of the room." But what
shocked Bobby most came at the end of the meeting. A representative of Dr. King took Bobby aside:

"I just want to say that Dr. King deeply appreciates the way
you handled the Birmingham affair."

"You watched these people attack me for over forty minutes and you didn't say a word. There is no point in your saying
this now," Bobby angrily retorted.

Professor John P. Roche, the National Chairman of Americans for Democratic Action, after studying the attitudes of John
F. Kennedy and those of Bobby, said that both men were "insen-
sitive to ideologies and political extremism. On the civil rights
issue the late President and the Attorney General initially considered Southern extremism as nothing more than a hard bargaining position."

In a Birmingham town hall, Bobby tried to moderate
between blacks and whites, hoping to get both races to settle on
a half a loaf for each. Profoundly shocked at the extremism of
the white Southerners, Bobby admitted that "it was like being
in a different country."

Chapter 14

A Tireless Attorney General

Bobby never rested on his laurels. He immediately buckled down to work. On the integration crisis in New Orleans, he phoned P. F. Gremillion, Louisiana's Attorney General, and told him that the Department of Justice intended to get Negro children into the all-white schools. Before Gremillion could answer, Bobby told him to come to Washington.

The State Legislature in New Orleans was trying to avoid school integration, by voting to stop advancing money for teacher salaries, forcing the black children to attend schools without teachers.

Bobby warned Governor Davis on legal action; he also told the local politicians that he would have his brother take actions that would be unpleasant for them. Surprisingly, the legislature voted the necessary funds to pay the teachers.

Bothered by what seemed rampant urban delinquency, Bobby set up a pilot project to determine the causes of juvenile delinquency. With a Congressional allocation of $618,000, Bobby moved to have 5,000 young people in federal jails questioned by Department of Justice staff people and social workers. Together with David Hacket, he went to New York City to talk to the Harlem gang leaders. With the reports in, the staff generated programs for the rehabilitation of both the underprivileged youngsters and those in the jails.

When he was accused of being ruthless, he answered flatly: "I'm not running a popularity contest. It doesn't matter if they like me or not. Jack can be nice to them. I don't try to antagonize people but somebody has to say no."

A reporter from *Look Magazine* once told Bobby that many people thought him "cold, ruthless and arrogant." When the reporter asked how he felt about the description, Bobby bluntly replied:

"If my children were old enough to understand I might be disturbed to have them find out what a mean father they have. I've had to step on some toes."

Never denying being the hatchet man for his brother, Bobby had to be tough towards those Southern politicians who had kept the blacks as second-class citizens for a hundred years. He meant to achieve this goal even it it meant using the executive power of the national government. Burke Marshall, the front-line commander, was assured support on behalf of civil rights for the blacks. Hardly two months in office, he became deeply involved in the "Negro problem." When he asked Congress for large sums of money to finance the civil rights program, the legislators wanted to know how he intended to use the funds: "To secure the Negroes right to vote," he answered, pointing out that 14 or 15 counties in the South with large Negro majorities did not have a single Negro representing them in Congress, because the number of voting blacks was pitifully small.

Bobby's secret of success lay in the staff he had chosen, men like Burke Marshall and John Siegenthaler on one hand, and on the other Harris Wofford, a former member of the staff of the Civil Rights Commission and now an assistant to the President; Berl Benhard, a classmate of Wofford at Yale, and John Field, the Executive Director of Vice President Johnson's Equal Opportunity Committee. Making themselves available to black leaders was an important part of their mission. "The direct accessibility of Bobby Kennedy, John Siegenthaler, and Burke Marshall," commented one black leader, through the simple act of a telephone call from a citizen in distress is no small achievement. I do not know how many little emergencies have been met in this way, but I have been told that they have taken place with more than occasional frequency."

Of greater importance was Bobby's direct connection to the White House. For the first time in the history of the nation, an Attorney General could rest assured that the President would not let him down.

Bobby wasn't playing games. Once, when the ultra-exclusive Metropolitan Club in Washington refused admittance to his black guest, Bobby immediately cancelled his membership.

Shortly after the incident, he made a check of all the divisions at the Justice Department and discovered that there were few Negro lawyers on staff. He quickly communicated with the deans of law schools, asking them to submit eligible blacks for Department jobs. In a few weeks he received a list of 150 black lawyers, and a year later, 50 were working in Bobby's department alone.

His increasing commitment to the cause of Negro rights was further demonstrated when he appointed Cecil Poole and

Merle McCurdy of Ohio and California to be United States Attorneys— the first Negroes ever appointed to such important positions.

He was also instrumental in getting Wade Hampton McGree and James B. Parsons appointed District Judges. A Negro became a Municipal Court justice in the District of Columbia. And Thurgood Marshall, General Counsel for the National Association for the Advancement of Colored People, was named to the United States Circuit Court, the second most important court in the land.

While Bobby was adding blacks to his own staff, Vice President Johnson, ably assisted by John Field, persuaded those contractors who did business with the government to take on more black workers. Acting on Bobby's suggestion, the President gave Johnson the necessary enforcement powers which enabled him to pressure businessmen into cooperating.

During the first six months of the Committee's existence, nine major companies agreed to hire Negroes. Fifty additional companies fell into line in the next half year. But when civil rights advocates urged that new laws be enacted to provide more safeguards, Bobby and the President did not respond with the decisiveness expected of them. Neither was willing to arouse the further ire of the Southern legislators, for they did not want to jeopardize the support they needed on foreign policy matters.

Despite Bobby's comparative moderation on the civil rights issue, he was the most hated man in the South. The Dixiecrats blamed him for all their troubles on one hand; the Negroes on the other considered him a "cold, calculating politician who would stick his neck out only so far."

The issue was picked up by Congressman Emanuel Celler of New York City and Senator Hugh Scott of Pennsylvania. They introduced bills in Congress designed to enforce civil rights, one of which would have quickened the pace in the desegregation of the schools, requiring all school boards to start action within six months, and calling for them to send their modus operandi to the Secretary of Health, Education and Welfare. It also empowered Bobby to serve injunctions to the school boards.

The Southern congressmen roared their disapproval for non compliance especially to the President. For fear the Confederate states would revolt again, he decided to withdraw his support for the Scott-Celler Bill.

In a communique, he stated that he had had no responsibility in the formulating of the bill nor in its introduction, making it painfully clear that the idea of the bill was the brainchild of Senator Scott and Emanuel Celler. All the while, Bobby stood strangely silent.

Although the Southerners were appeased, the liberals and the Negroes felt betrayed by the two Kennedy brothers.

With Washington in an uproar, Bobby kept busy with many local problems. In Richmond, Virginia, he ordered the re-opening of the public schools in Prince Edward County whose schools had been shut down for a long period. Bobby and his traveling operatives were also putting pressure on business leaders in Memphis, Dallas, Atlanta and other Southern cities to get them behind the school desegregation movement, threatening them with punitive action if they did not comply.

In the area of Negro rights, nevertheless, Bobby got more than a passing grade. In his record on civil liberties, on the other hand, Bobby never rated high.

The American Civil Liberties Union was in conflict with Bobby on more than one occasion. It opposed his wiretap bill which permitted government agencies to use wiretap evidence in cases of national security and kidnapping. Among others, the bill made it necessary to get the approval of a federal Judge to use the evidence gained by wiretap.

Congressman Celler, then Chairman of the House Judiciary Committee, was one of the men responsible for the defeat of the bill. He did not want that much power in the hands of the Attorney General, who, under the bill, could determine exactly what constituted a national emergency.

Bobby also favored the Walter Immigration Bill which would deny due process to aliens seeking to delay deportation.

He simply did not comprehend the essence of civil liberties. A Boston Irishman— an *ethnic* himself— he was always in the forefront in the battle for economic justice but he never waged a good fight for libertarian ideas, voting for a New Deal legislator, but always rejecting those ideas affecting the civil liberties of the nation's citizens. John F. Kennedy developed a greater regard for civil liberties as he matured; Bobby, like many of his compatriots in Boston, found it difficult to fight for these same liberties.

It is interesting that while writer Gore Vidal insisted that Bobby would "never" comprehend the issue of civil liberties, Arthur Schlesinger Jr. believed that Bobby would have eventually developed into one of the country's outstanding liberals.

Chapter 15

Racial Strife in Dixie

Tension had been mounting in the South for a long time. On May 22, 1961, Reverend Martin Luther King, Jr. and his Freedom Riders huddled in the first Baptist Church in Montgomery, Alabama, singing religious hymns; outside a mob threatened to break into the church. Bobby quickly dispatched 150 Federal Marshals to protect the embattled group of men and women.

"These people are scared— and I don't blame them," Bobby shouted to his assistants, fearing that if something were to happen to Dr. King, his brother's Administration could be destroyed. Worse, the nation itself could go down.

He tried to convince the black leaders to concentrate first and foremost on getting their people to vote; then to test their rights to travel in desegregated public conveyances. Although many black leaders suspected that Bobby was more concerned with the feelings of white Southerners than seeing that justice prevailed, the fact remained that Bobby supported the Supreme Court ruling which made public inter-state transportation facilities equally available to all.

It was ironic that the crisis should have arisen in Alabama where the governor, known as a racket buster, worked with Bobby on the McClellan (Rackets) Committee, and they had become close friends. In fact, Governor Patterson was one of the very few Southern politicians who supported the candidacy of Kennedy. "We got along very well," Bobby recalled when relations between them deteriorated. "Patterson was our first break in the solid South."

On May 4, 12 black and white Freedom Riders took a bus from Washington D.C. to the South to test the reaction of white Southerners. They drove through Virginia, North Carolina and Georgia without incident until they arrived at Rock Hill, South Carolina. There a mob attacked them, beating three of the men. When the Riders arrived in Atlanta, they formed a splinter group to travel by Greyhound Bus to Annistone, Alabama, where a mob of heavily-armed men waited alongside the road.

About six miles west of Anniston, the mob stopped the bus and destroyed it with a fire bomb, injuring most of the Riders.

In Birmingham, a Trailways Bus of Riders was attacked by another mob. Although the FBI had warned the Police Department that there was a danger of a riot, no policeman was in sight until 10 minutes after the mob had done its ugly work. The chief of police later gave the reason for the absence: it was Mother's Day.

Now Bobby had a problem to resolve: to find a bus driver willing to drive the Riders to safety. He phoned a number of local people; finally, he was referred to a Mr. Cruit, a local official of the Greyhound Bus Company, who, without telling Bobby, had recorded the conversation:

Kennedy: Mr. Cruit, this is the Attorney General. I just talked to Manning. Isn't there some way we can get this bus to Montgomery?

Cruit: No sir, I don't have a man to drive the bus. They are fearful of their lives and refuse to drive the bus under any conditions... My union men tell me that none of their men will take the bus out.

Kennedy: What union is that?

Cruit: The Amalgamated Association of Street, Electrical etc., Local Division No. 1314.

Kennedy: Well, hell, you can look for one, can't you? After all, these people have tickets and are entitled to transportation to continue their trip to Montgomery... Well, surely, somebody in the damn bus company can drive a bus, can't they?

Cruit: No sir, we are in the advertising end of the operation and only drivers are allowed to drive a bus.

Kennedy: Don't you have any school bus drivers around there who would be willing to drive a bus that few miles?

Cruit responded by saying that he could not permit any unqualified driver to handle a vehicle worth $46,000. Bobby advised Cruit to contact the company and to get the bus moving.

The recorded conversation was later released by Cruit and his associates. They wanted to prove that Bobby had planned the Freedom Rider project himself in order to embarrass the South. Later questioned by Ray Moore, the News Director of WSB-TV-Atlanta, Bobby told him that he had first received the information about the bus trip *after* the vehicle had been destroyed in Anniston, on May 15. On Monday, he had attempted to contact Governor Patterson but was unable to reach him. When he was asked if he had plotted "to embarrass the South", he declared that it "is completely untrue."

When asked why he had sent Federal Marshals into the

town instead of troops, Bobby answered: "Because I didn't think troops were necessary. I thought the marshals could do the job. I was against sending troops."

Then he was asked whether he had encouraged or discouraged the Freedom Riders: "There was a discussion during the week before the Montgomery incident that occurred between my representative and the Freedom Riders to try to get them not to make these trips. If there had been a concentrated effort on the part of the authorities in Alabama we wouldn't have had to send the marshals there. And I think I would have been derelict in my responsibilities if I had not ordered them in. I have no apology to make."

On May 18, another group of Riders arrived in Birmingham where they were hustled off to jail by none other than Eugene T. (Bull) Connor, the one who had let vicious police dogs loose on helpless blacks. Although Connor shipped the Riders to Tennessee, they returned at high noon, but were immediately hemmed in by 18 highway patrolmen cruising the entire length of the road, backed by a plane flying overhead. The mob walked through the city, beating news photographers and a number of innocent bystanders. After a few hours, the State Police, with the Sheriff's posse, moved in to disperse the rioters.

On May 21, a group of Federal marshals under Byron White, U.S. Deputy Attorney General, was flown to the Maxwell Air Force Base. When a mob intended to invade the church where Dr. King was conducting a meeting, 400 policemen moved in to establish order.

Governor Patterson declared martial law, replacing federal marshals with National Guards. On May 24, the Riders departed from Montgomery to Jackson, Mississippi, protected by highway patrolmen, 3 reconnaissance planes, 2 helicopters. 1,000 National Guardsmen patrolled the route leading into the city. On arriving, the Riders tried to enter the segregated restrooms at the terminal and were placed under arrest "for disturbing the peace." Outside, a mob of whites beat blacks aimlessly. A veritable riot was underway.

"It's just terrible, terrible, terrible, fists... thugs, they're bleeding... there's not a cop in sight... they're beating 'em now. It's terrible," Doad reported to Burke Marshall in Washington.

When Byron White tried to reach Bobby at his home in McLean, Virginia, he was told that Bobby was out horseback riding. On his return, he immediately phoned White. On getting an initial report, Bobby cut him short to call his brother at the White House. A few minutes later, he called White again, ordering U.S. Marshals to the strife-torn town.

Bobby sent a telegram to Governor Patterson, outlining the week's happenings, reminding him that he had given his solemn oath to cooperate with the federal government.

The small army of agents were now mending their way to Montgomery under Byron White. Bobby also ordered the FBI to intensify its investigation of the rioters, asking Federal District Judge Frank M. Johnson, Jr. to issue an injunction to restrain the hatemongering organizations from "interfering with peaceful interstate commerce or travel on buses."

Bobby and the President were boiling mad at what appeared to be Governor Patterson's refusal to deal with the crisis. The Governor was both embarrassed and angry.

"Your action," Patterson shouted to White, "is illegal, unconstitutional and worsening the situation, and it's an insult to the great State of Alabama."

Bobby used the telephone with the dexterity of a piano virtuoso, speaking to White in Montgomery and to the Negro leaders as well as local officials, staying in his office until Sunday morning, July 21. When he finally went to bed, he really thought the trouble had subsided. He was wrong.

He had tried to convince Dr. King to stay out of the town, but the Reverend had told him that he would not shirk his responsibilities towards his people, adding that he would stay on and face whatever was in store.

The mob was on the loose again in Montgomery. Governor Patterson called Bobby in Washington and bellowed that he was responsible for encouraging the Freedom Riders safari into the deep South.

"You sent them down here," he shouted. Bobby remained calm.

"You know it isn't true," Bobby retorted. "I don't care if that's what you tell your people down there on television, John, but don't tell me that."

Patterson was overwrought. He accused Bobby of "engineering" the entire project, saying that in his opinion and that of the National Guard Commander, King and his people could not be safeguarded from the enraged citizens outside the church. The remark about the Commander aroused Bobby's anger.

"I want *him* to say that to me. I want to hear a General in the United States say he can't protect Martin Luther King." Taken aback by Bobby's intensity, Patterson promised to do what he could to save King.

The long night of *knives* was at an end at last. Dr. King and his Freedom Riders were finally escorted out of the church early Monday morning. Not having any faith in Governor Patterson's promises, Bobby dispatched 200 additional federal officers into the city.

In Washington D.C., government officials became disturbed over the possibility of violence breaking out in other cities. Bobby asked Dr. King to call off further demonstrations until the situation could be controlled more effectively. But Dr. King did not agree.

Later, Dr. King told Guthman that this was "the turning point and a testing point. Little Rock was the psychological turning point as far as school segregation was concerned. If we can break the back of the opposition here [in Alabama] public facilities will be desegregated tomorrow."

Bobby and Dr. King were two men from different worlds. They were able to find a basis of agreement in the over-all objectives which called for first-class citizenship for the blacks. They did not agree on the tactics. Dr. King had been born to struggle for justice; Bobby never had had to face that kind of situation. When the Irish were ostracized in Boston by the local Brahmins— *"Irish need not apply"* was the most many of them had to endure— Joe simply moved his family to New York where they were accepted as equals. For the blacks, "They will use their lives and their bodies to right a wrong," Dr. King said with deep emotion.

Bobby became irritated. He was worried about America's image abroad, certain that it was being sullied by the events taking place in the South. When Dr. King said that the racist feelings prevalent in the nation would eventually "destroy the soul of the country," Bobby lost his patience.

They approached the crisis from different positions. King, a man of peace, felt that the Negroes would only achieve their goals by demonstrating, contending that their rights would not be granted without pressure. Bobby, however, was certain that the Establishment would in time grant those rights, assuring Dr. King that the government was powerful enough to enforce them. What occurred later confirmed Dr. King's opinion.

Governor Ross Barnett defied the government after he had promised Washington that he intended to cooperate in getting James Meredith accepted as a student at Mississippi University. As expected, the mob rioted and murdered three civil rights activists. It did not prevent the local inhabitants from beating the blacks, the federal marshals and others. A French newspaperman was killed during one fracas.

When Bobby was later asked what he and the government had accomplished, he answered:

"I think that in two areas particularly controversial, we

made some progress— civil rights and organized crime. We made greater progress than I had anticipated in the area of organized crime. In civil rights we had great accomplishments, in spite of the bitterness and hatred... This is important."

In a sense that was true. But he was conveniently forgetting his own responsibility in allowing J. Edgar Hoover to accuse Dr. King of every crime in the book.

On October 18, 1963, Alan Belmont, the Assistant Director of the FBI, with Hoover's enthusiastic approval, distributed a document discrediting King, entitled *Communism and the Negro Movement— A Current Analysis,* drafted by William Sullivan, another FBI operator. The publication went to key staff at the White House and to various executive officers of the government. The unexpected attack, however, outraged the Attorney General. Bobby immediately ordered the document withdrawn.

Hoover was determined to destroy Dr. King's reputation. In a staff meeting lasting 9 hours, he came up with blueprints of future operations against Dr. King. It was at that conclave that Sullivan suggested replacing King with Samuel P. Pierce Jr., a prominent lawyer who had never been active in the civil rights movement. *Crazy Billy,* as Sullivan was called by his colleagues at the FBI, had written a letter addressed to his superior, Alan Belmont, on January 8, 1964 to that effect.

The ill-advised sanction to place taps on Dr. King's telephones caused Bobby a lot of embarrassment.

In November 1964, William Sullivan sent the edited tapes to Coretta King. An anonymous letter was also mailed from Tampa, Florida:

"There is only one thing left for you to do to prevent the release of the tapes in 34 days. You had better take it before your filthy fraudulent self is bared to the nation." (It was the time when Dr. King was going to be awarded the Nobel Prize.

The Hoover character assassination attempts could have been stopped had Bobby not allowed those tapes.

In learning of Hoover's activities, Dr. King responded in his usual quiet manner: "The Director has apparently faltered under the burdens of his office."

Chapter 16

The Bay of Pigs

Bobby not only functioned as the Attorney General, he also doubled in brass as his older brother's adviser on foreign policy.

Allen Dulles and Richard Bisell, two top CIA men, went to Joe Kennedy's palatial estate in Palm Beach to brief the President about the planned invasion of Cuba, and to ask for the green light.

While Eisenhower was President, training camps were established for a future invasion of Cuba, as Castro's pilots were being trained to fly MIG fighters in Czechoslovakia, and the latest Russian combat planes were being transported in crates to Havana.

Although the situation was dangerous, Kennedy was well aware of Article 15 of the Charter of the Organization of American States: "No state or group of states has the right to intervene directly or indirectly for any reason whatever in the internal affairs of any state."

If Kennedy, therefore, were to order an attack, the Latin Americans would be up in arms; if he didn't, he would have betrayed the American voters to whom he had promised that if elected President he would not permit "the establishment of a Communist base 90 miles off the Florida coast." In one of his speeches, Kennedy baited Richard Nixon because Nixon had been urging the United States to stand up to Khrushchev and for not having the courage to control Castro. In another, he promised to assist the exiled Cubans to overthrow Castro: "While we cannot violate international law we must recognize that these rebels represent the real voice of Cuba." And in another, he said that "if we extend the hand of American friendship in a common effort to wipe out poverty and discontent and hopelessness in which communism feeds— only then will we drive back tyranny until it ultimately perishes in the streets of Havana."

Charles Bowles, the former advertising man and U.S. statesman, was amazed by the news of the planned invasion. He gave Dean Rusk a memorandum explaining why he was opposed to it. But Rusk disagreed because, in his view, it would not involve many men. Senator Fulbright told the President that the "Castro regime is a thorn in the flesh but it is not a dagger in the heart," and he denounced those who were calling for an attack on Cuba.

Bobby approached Arthur Schlesinger concerning the pending invasion: "I hear you don't think much of this business," Bobby commented. And after he listened to the reasons why Schlesinger opposed it, Bobby added: "You may be right or wrong, but the President has made up his mind. Don't push it any further. Now is the time for everyone to stand by the President."

The project, first formulated by the Eisenhower Administration on March 17, 1960, was now in full swing. CIA operators were secretly instructing the recruits in the intricacies of guerilla warfare. Another contingent of Cubans received its training in Louisiana. When it was shipped to Guatemala, however, a local newspaper revealed the planned "secret" invasion of Cuba— October 30, 1960.

Although the following January was a most embarrassing month for the CIA, it proved to be an illuminating one for President Kennedy. The majority of the Cubans air-dropped into the Escambray Mountains either were killed or captured, and the population—which was to have revolted against Castro—did not.

With the initial invasion thwarted, the CIA stepped up its recruitment to mount another invasion.

On being told by Bisell and Dulles that Cuban pilots would soon go back to Cuba in large numbers, President Kennedy went on television: "If we don't move now, Mr. Castro may become a much greater danger than he is to us today."

A week before the operation, Kennedy asked for and received a written endorsement from General Lemnitzer and Admiral Arleigh Burke, and verbal assents of Rusk and McNamara. At a press conference Rusk said: "The American people are entitled to know whether we are intervening in Cuba or intend to do so in the future. The answer to that question is no. What happens in Cuba is for Cubans to decide."

On April 4, the President called a special meeting to discuss the invasion. Among those present were Dean Rusk, Robert McNamara, Douglas Dillon, Allen Dulles, General Lemnitzer, Tom Nann, Paul Nitze, Adolph Berle, McGeorge Bundy, Arthur Schlesinger, Robert Bissel, Senator Fulbright, Richard Goodwin, and Robert Kennedy. Bissell, a former professor of economics and the one who had planned the U-2 flights over Russia as well as the overthrow of the Arbentz Government in Guatemala, spoke first. He said Cuba was ripe for revolution: "This invasion will be successful." Dulles agreed by adding that the invasion was bound to succeed.

The President walked around the room pointing his finger at each man. Each answering in the positive, until he pointed to Senator Fulbright, who denounced the plan, saying that such intervention was unworthy of a democratic nation. Schlesinger, on the other hand, said nothing at all. Later he wrote a memo addressed to the President expressing his doubts about the venture. Adolph Berle shouted: "Let 'em rip!", and concluded with the following statement: "A power confrontation with the Communists in this hemisphere [is] ultimately inevitable and it might as well come immediately."

Bobby's sole concern was the kind of an image the country would be projecting. He didn't relish the idea of a sneak attack— a sort of Pearl Harbor in reverse, but was committed.

On April 12, the President assured the American people that "there will not be under any circumstances an intervention in Cuba by the Unites States forces."

On the day of the invasion, the President was at Glen Ora with his wife and children, paying a visit to Daniel C. Sands at his 200-acre farm where they watched some of the horse races. Bobby, meanwhile, was in Williamsburg, Virginia delivering a speech.

With the initial phase of the invasion gone bad, Bissell and General Charles Cabell urged Rusk to talk to the President about a second air strike. He told them instead to do it themselves.

Amidst the Cuban disaster, Russia and China began to intensify the Laos situation, while the Berlin *boil* looked as if it was about to burst. Realizing the international dangers, Kennedy decided not to commit any of his forces to a Cuban invasion.

Castro's combat flyers scored direct hits on the ships carrying munitions, and also shot down 6 B-26 planes.

With the invasion an apparent disaster, Adlai Stevenson tried to lighten the gloomy atmosphere with his usual humor for the U.S. delegation to the U.N. He said that he was not certain who was attacking Cuba, but sure of who was attacking us. Needless to say, the joke didn't go down too well.

Catching the U.S. with its pants down, Raul Roa, the Cuban Ambassador to the UN, gave a detailed blueprint of the American involvement: named names, said that Bender-nee Droller was the CIA agent who handled the operation, and revealed the story of the Guatemala encampment, the recruiting of the Cuban exiles, and the cover stories used by the CIA. Stevenson muttered it wasn't so, but nobody believed him. The nation's most highly-respected international figure had been exposed as a liar. For the second time, the American people learned that they had been lied to. First, there was the U-2 incident, now the invasion. Pierre Salinger, the President's press secretary, played dumb: "All we know about Cuba is what we read on the wire services." Bobby also showed no concern. But when things began to surface, he got angry.

Coincidental with the announcement of the defeat of the Cuban invasion, a grand reception was taking place at the White House, a gala given to honor senators, congressmen and their wives. At 10:15 p.m., President and Mrs. Kennedy appeared in the ballroom to the music of the Marine Band playing a spirited, *Mr. Wonderful.* The President and the exquisitely dressed Jackie whirled around the ballroom, while other couples began dancing. Bobby and Ethel stood to one side, somber looking, oppressed by the tragedy enfolding on Cuban beaches.

After a dinner of chicken-a-la-king and pheasant, the President asked to be excused. Bobby followed a few minutes later, telling Ethel his brother needed him.

Although the battle was lost, CIA agent Bissell still asked the President to order the Air Force into the fray, assuring Kennedy that the jet fighters aboard the *Essex* together with the B-26 from Puerto Cabezas would be more than enough to wipe out Castro's army. Rusk did not believe that American air power was a good idea. Admiral Arleigh Burke asked the President to order the commander of the cruiser *Essex* to pour heavy gunfire into the Castro troop concentration near the beaches. When General Lenmitzer concurred with Burke's suggestion, the President allowed Navy units to fly over the Bay of Pigs for an hour. Jets would support the B-26 in their ground strikes. The Navy planes would be ordered to fly between the B-26 and Castro's jets and fire at them if they attacked any United States planes. The basic idea was to use the Navy jets as bait to lure Castro's pilots into attacking them.

The ensuing events proved all those assumptions wrong. Bobby was concerned with his brother's state of depression, knowing that there would not be one single person courageous enough to stick his neck out and give an honest opinion.

The President asked himself how he could have been so far off base. "All my life I've known better than to depend on experts. How could I have been so stupid as to let them go ahead?"

Suddenly he thought that he had made a mistake placing Bobby at Justice where Byron White might have done just as well: "Bobby should be with the CIA. I must have someone there with whom I can be in complete and intimate contact— someone from whom I know I will be getting the right pitch."

The CIA and the Army Chiefs of Staff may have misled the President, but in the last analysis it was he who made the final decision to invade Cuba. Months after the fiasco, he continued to speak his heart out to all those who saw him. One evening, he told Paul Fay that he resented the criticism heaped upon him by those who wanted to commit American troops in the battle:

"Nobody is going to force me to do anything I don't think is in the best interests of the country. I'll never compromise the principles on which this country is built because a fanatical fringe in this country puts so-called national pride above national reason." Anguished, he continued: "Do you think I'm going to carry on my conscience the responsibility for the wanton killing and maiming of children like our children we saw here this evening? Do you think I'm going to cause a nuclear exchange for that? Because I was forced into doing something that I didn't think was proper and right? Well, if you or anybody else thinks I am, he's crazy."

Chapter 17
Bobby and the Taylor Committee

The Bay of Pigs fiasco provided the Republicans with appropriate ammunition. Although the President took full responsibility for the defeat, he was determined to discover what had gone wrong, and why the CIA had so ill-advised the Government.

Bobby suggested that a committee be formed with General Maxwell Taylor, to include Admiral Arleigh Burke and Allen Dulles, who had been responsible for the Bay of Pigs.

Two Cubans, Pepe San Roman and Blas Casares, who had participated in the invasion, came to the capital to offer their testimony. General Taylor asked questions to learn how Castro's men had reacted under fire, how many of the invaders had been killed, and what the total losses of Castro's army were. Bobby, on the other hand, was interested in learning about the reaction of the civilians.

The two men gave him the facts as they saw them, adding that three or possibly four more jet fighters might have spelled the difference between victory and defeat.

Bobby asked who had fought on the beaches and what the CIA had promised. San Roman declared that they had been told they would get more air support. On being asked about the operation, Casares said that those responsible for the planning of the invasion must have been insane. Amused by the remark, Bobby, General Taylor and Admiral Burke roared with laughter; Dulles, however, did not think it that funny.

The questioning completed, Bobby took the Cubans to the White House. After San Roman, the spokesman for his group, gave the President a brief account of the battle, Bobby invited them to his house. Ethel surprised everyone with her questions about the invasion to the point of embarrassing her husband, especially when she talked about the lack of planes.

The Bobby-Taylor Committee concluded that the CIA underestimated the strength of the Castro air force, that his army was efficient, and that no less than 10,000 highly-trained soldiers could have won the war. Further, the report stated that the tactical groundwork was unbelievably bad, the choice of the invasion site wrong, and there weren't enough supply ships on hand.

After studying the report, Bobby concluded that "victory was never close," promising that "The President won't assume anything from now on. Simply because a man is supposed to be an expert in the field will not qualify him to the President."

Walter Lippman, critical of McGeorge Bundy and Walt Rostow, thought that the President had been led down the garden path. He also said that Arthur Schlesinger Jr. and Dean Rusk should have voiced their opinions loud and clear at that crucial meeting on April 15. The eminent pundit was also critical of the attitudes of Dulles, Bissell, General Lenmitzer, Admiral Burke and Adolph Berle, implying they should be sacked.

Since the Chief Executive under our constitutional system cannot resign, the men serving as advisors should have born the major responsibility. Lippman, incidentally, did not mention Bobby, mainly because Bobby had been against the *sneak attack* on Cuba. And of course there was the sole exception of Senator Fulbright.

With the Republicans making hay, Bobby agreed to an interview with *U.S. News and World Report:* "There was never any plans made for the U.S. air cover, so there was nothing to withdraw. [Air cover] was never seriously suggested by the military... [and] never been considered... In the planning, it was never contemplated that there be U.S. air cover. The President didn't withdraw air cover for the landing forces."

According to his version, an air attack was "made on Saturday on Cuban airports." Bobby was talking about the attack which Stevenson believed had been waged causing a flurry at the UN and elsewhere, which showed a United States participation. These allegations created embarrassment in Washington. The *flurry,* Bobby called it, was his way of describing how the UN delegates reacted to the involvement and the use of Stevenson as a respectable "front man" to cover the White House's role.

Bobby admitted that another attack had been scheduled, but because of the reaction on this matter, the President "gave instructions that it should not take place at that time unless those responsible felt that it was so important it had to take place, in which case they should call him and discuss it further."

Bobby kept insisting that it wasn't the air cover over the beaches that had been a subject of discussion. He told the reporter that "the attacks on the airport took place later that day."

He also said that the men who piloted the B-26 from Central America were on the job. Those were the planes, according to him, "that were supposed to be utilized," admitting later, "they proved inadequate." He also felt that it was not due to "any last minute decision of the President or anyone else."

When the reporter asked Bobby who had been responsible for the planning of the invasion, he said it had been the Pentagon, the Joint Chiefs of Staff and the CIA. He also told the reporter thet "the President had made it clear [that] no American manpower, air power or American ships would be used."

After several months of deliberations, the Taylor committee was unable to arrive at an agreement on the cause of the fiasco. Towards the end of 1962, Robert Hilsman, the State Department's Director of Intelligence and Research, prepared a *White Paper*, based on the findings of the Taylor Committee. McGeorge Bundy and Pierre Salinger urged the President to release the report to the public, but Bobby disagreed. When Sorensen asked the President to allow a distinguished writer to have access to the files, he said, "This isn't the time. Besides, we want to tell the story ourselves."

Some of the Committee's conclusions did leak out. Bobby and General Taylor agreed that the original plan for the invasion of Cuba had been poor in concept and that the military action had been doomed from its very inception. Admiral Burke still insisted that the second strike would have been successful. Taking a middle position, Dulles said that the CIA and the military should have had an alternate plan.

One result of the investigation was the easing out of both Dulles and Bissell as directors of the CIA. John McCone, a very conservative businessman who had amassed a large fortune building ships for the government during World War II, was appointed director. Richard Helm, who was later to display a special penchant to write the "wrong kind" of letters, one of which was critical about Johnson's foreign policies, replaced Bissell.

A few months after the defeat, Bobby admitted it would have been far wiser not to have ordered the invasion. He also added that his brother had learned a very bitter lesson: never again to listen and take the advice from so-called experts. What the American people in general and their politicians in particular may not have learned is that in dealing with such volatile situations as Castro's Cuba, one either takes the full, necessary actions to secure victory or not participate at all. And of the courses, the latter would be preferable.

The government's role in the episode was best summed up by Stewart Alsop: "Trouble was that we were acting like an old whore and trying to pretend that we were just the sweet young girl we used to be."

Chapter 18

The Case of the Missing American Flyers

Bobby dabbled in everything that concerned his brother. When Senator Everett McKinley Dirksen revealed that four American airmen had been killed in the action, it became a foregone conclusion that he would be involved.

Dirksen's revelations on the floor of the Senate proved to be highly embarrassing. The President had remarked some time before that "the government will do every thing it possibly can and I think it can meet its responsibilities to make sure that there are no Americans involved in any actions inside Cuba."

On January 21, 1963, Bobby was interviewed by a reporter of *U.S. News and World Report*. He said that "noAmericans died in the Bay of Pigs action."

The wives of the 4 missing flyers had not seen nor heard from their husbands and were worried about them. Before the case was solved, many important government officials, including Bobby, would be caught in a welter of lies.

Thomas Willard Ray, Leo Francis Baker, Riley W. Shamburger Jr., and Wade Carroll Gray had piloted two B-26s. On April 19, 1961, they had all been shot down. The men had been recruited by Alex E. Carlson, a lawyer, who maintained an office at 145 Curtis Parkway, Miami Springs, Florida. The office had been leased in the name of the Double-Check Corporation, which, on May 4, 1959 had established itself as a broad-based business, with Carlson as its president, and Earl Sanders vice-president, Margery Carlson as secretary-treasurer, and Wesley R. Pillsburg as its local director. The company's chief function was to serve as a cover for the CIA for the recruiting of trained pilots.

Assisted by General Reid Doster, top brass of the Alabama Air National Guard, and Major David W. Hutchinson, chief of the 9th Tactical Air Force, Calrson stumbled on a veritable treasure-trove of seasoned pilots in Alabama, Virginia and Arkansas units of the Air National Guard. Before leaving for parts unknown, the 24 recruited pilots were told to have their wives write in care of Joseph Greenland, Box 7924, Main Post Office, Chicago Illinois, a CIA drop.

The pilots Ray and Baker were shot down down over Cuban soil; the other two over water as a result of a confusion in time schedules on the part of the operational officers who allowed the pilots to fly unprotected over Cuba after the Navy jets had returned to their carrier.

On April 19, 1961, Castro announced the American air raid over Cuba, reporting that Cubans had the body of Leo Francis Bell together with documents listing his flight license number, his social security and motor vehicle registration number, and his address at 48 Beacon Street, Boston, Massachusetts. The documents were of course fakes; the CIA had prepared them for just such a contingency. In any event, the flyer's real name was Leo Baker.

On April 26, Margaret Ray received a visit from Thomas R. McDowell, a respected Birmingham lawyer, accompanied aby an unidentified man. They told her that her husband's C-46, a transport plane, had plunged into the sea, and that her husband was probably dead.

On May 4, at a press conference in Birmingham, Carlson told the reporters that the four missing men had flown from a Central American airstrip and that their engine had concked out, resulting in their crashing into the sea with all hands aboard presumably drowned, adding that the pilots knew what they were in for when they accepted the jobs, insinuating that they were mercenaries, and admitting that his corporation had hired them on behalf of a Cuban anti-Castro organization.

In an attempt to appease the wives, Carlson sent checks to them for $225 each and later increased the amount to $245.

But Mrs. Shamburger, the mother of the dead pilot, resented Carlson's remarks. She wanted to learn the truth about her son. She wrote to Denman F. Stanfield, the State Department's Director for the Protection and Representation Division, who assured the distraught mother that he would make a serious search on the whereabouts of her missing son. She received a letter from Major Sidney Ormerod of the U.S. Air Force, Division of Administration Services, telling her that he was unable to find anything about her son's "accident," stating that Riley Shamburger was not "on active duty in his military status," and suggesting that she communicate with the Hayes Aircraft Corporation in Birmingham where her son had been employed.

Far from being discouraged, she wrote to John McCone, the new chief of the CIA. In due time, she received a letter signed by a Lieutenant General Marshall S. Carter, Acting Director of the U.S. Army. Expressing deep sympathy, he informed the bewildered mother that the CIA was at a loss to furnish any additional information, adding that the inquiry had been conducted in a very thorough manner but that he did not come up with encouraging answers. She now wrote to President Kennedy, and Brigadier General Godfrey T. McHugh, the Air Force aide at the White House, responded: "... no agency in Washington including the CIA possesses the slightest pertinent information about your son's disappearance."

Finally on February 25, 1963, she learned from Senator Dirksen what had really happened to her son.

In Washington that day, many faces were red. David Kraslow, a byliner on the Knight newspapers, on January 21, 1963, had interviewed Bobby, who had said that no Americans had been killed during the Bay of Pigs engagement. Bobby's Air Force aide had also told Mrs. Shamburger that no one in the capital knew what had happened to the flyer.

"If no Americans were involved, where is my son?" she asked.

Chapter 19

More Trouble

Bobby was putting in 16 hours a day, working inhuman hours while the Taylor Committee investigated the invasion. During the early morning hours, he studied data at CIA headquarters; later, he was at the White House discussing foreign policy with his brother; and at night, he was at his office functioning as the nation's Attorney General. Of all these activities, those dealing with Foreign Affairs interested him the most.

On receiving word that the Soviets were constructing the *wall* separating East from West Berlin, he quickly conferred with his President brother.

Although Rusk was the Secretary of State, Bobby did most of the talking with Soviet Ambassador Mikhail Menshikov, and appearing on the television program *Meet the Press* he reiterated the Administration's position that West Berlin would be protected. On being asked how far the government intended to go to keep West Berlin out of the hands of the Soviets, Bobby answered matter-of-factly: "If it comes to that [the President] will use nuclear weapons."

At a later date, Bobby revealed the President's feelings about nuclear war: "It doesn't really matter as far as you and I are concerned. What really matters are the children."

While Bobby was working on getting more involved on the international scene, at home the specter of the Cuban crisis remained.

With 1,113 prisoners surviving the Bay of Pigs, Castro proposed to exchange them for 500 tractors and bulldozers. A *Tractor for Freedom Committee* was organized with Eleanor Roosevelt and a number of other notables on board, its purpose to raise the necessary funds. Many congressional leaders, however, criticised the Committee, for they believed that the machinery would strengthen the Cuban economy. Unable to raise the required sum, the Committee eventually disbanded, and the exchange did not take place.

Castro, meanwhile, released 60 wounded prisoners pursuant to a pledge by the Cuban Family Committee for the Liberation of War Prisoners, Inc. to pay him $2,500,000 in ransom money.

The release did not appease the Cuban community in Miami. Bobby, who had frequently met with Cuban leaders, knew that their compatriots were in a white heat because of the meager results achieved in gaining the release of the Bay of Pigs veterans. Nildo Acevedo and Manuel Reboso, two of the released Cubans, talked to Robert Hurwick, a State Department functionary in charge of prisoner problems. Sensing that Hurwick had little concern about the fate of the prisoners, Acevedo and Reboso together with Roberto San Roman, went over to the Justice Department to see Bobby. In an emotional tone, San Roman told Bobby that the Miami community had become cynical about the government's attitude towards the prisoners, afraid that Castro was going to execute them. Bobby assured San Roman that he would do everything possible to save the men, and to be in daily contact until the situation was resolved.

A short time later, Bobby met Enrique Ruiz Williams, another of the recently released prisoners. Bobby told him to hire a professional fund-raiser to secure the money necessary to ransom the prisoners. Eventually, Lucius Clay headed the Cuban Families Committee; but the rich Cubans didn't contribute much.

Bobby suggested to get James Donovan to serve as a negotiator. A Brooklyn lawyer, Donovan had successfully secured the exchange of Francis Gary Powers, the U-2 pilot, and Frederick L. Pryor, an American student held by the Soviets for Colonel Rudolph Abel, the masterspy. As Donovan had never met Bobby, he asked Enrique Ruiz Williams to arrange an appointment. At a meeting on July 2, Bobby persuaded Donovan to act as counsel for the Cuban Families Committee. In actuality, both Donovan and the Committee would be serving as fronts for the U.S. Government in the negotiations with Castro for the release of the prisoners.

Donovan went to Cuba where he told Castro of his inability to get the tractors or the bulldozers, but that he could could convince the U.S. Government to ship medicine and baby food to Havana. Although Castro accepted the substitute offer, he insisted that the money promised for the release of the 60 wounded prisoners be paid immediately. On this note, Donovan went to see John E. McKeen, President of Charles Pfizer Company, and John T. Connor, head of Merck, Sharp and Dohme. Both promised to donate the drugs.

While Donovan and Castro were about to conclude an agreement for the release of the prisoners, a U-2 plane photographed a Russian missile site. In spite of the profound implications, Donovan discovered that Castro was still interested in making a deal.

With the talks in progress, Bobby became involved in the missile crisis. Senator Keating, Republican legislator from New York, was making loud noises about the missiles installed by the Russians. President Kennedy said that Keating was exaggerating the danger, explaining that the Soviets were only installing anti-missiles and short-range rockets and that the United States was not in danger of being attacked. The President and Bobby knew Keating was telling the truth, but could not afford to frighten the American people. When on October 4, the U-2 boat revealed the missiles were MRBM's capable of hitting cities 1,200 miles away from Cuba, the President decided to act.

For the next two weeks, the Administration remained in session. To avoid journalists, the men entered the White House from a side door, for it was important not to have the public know how serious a crisis they were confronting. Among those at the sessions were Dean Rusk, Robert McNamara, Lyndon Johnson, McGeorge Bundy, Douglas Dillon, General Maxwell Taylor, John McCone, George W. Ball, Rosewell L. Gilpatrick, Llwellyn Thompson, Teodore Sorensen, Edward M. Martin, George Andersen, and Robert F. Kennedy.

On October 17, the Administration, certain the Russians were constructing launching sites, concluded that definite action had to be taken. One suggested a surprise attack. Bobby reiterated it "would be a Pearl Harbor in reverse." The President agreed with Bobby.

The President first let the Russians know that the missiles had to be taken out of Cuba or else, then he advised the public to prepare for war. Meanwhile, Russian ships en-route to Cuba were intercepted by American warships. Finally on October 26, Khrushchev made known his intentions to avert hostilities. Soon after, in another note, the Russian leader offered to remove the missiles if the Americans would dismantle their missile sites in Turkey. Bobby suggested to ignore the second letter and to respond only to the first one. Khrushchev ordered the missiles withdrawn. The U.S., on the other hand, took the Jupiter missiles out of Turkey, and promised not to invade Cuba.

While helping the President resolve the missile crisis, Bobby kept up the prisoner negotiations. From Alvaro Sanchez, he learned that the Kennedy brothers stood so high with the American people that they could get anything they wanted. Public opinion, the Cubans contented, would be overwhelmingly in favor of an arrangement with Castro to release the prisoners. Bobby agreed and predicted that they would be on American soil in the near future. He also met with other leaders to tell them that an agreement was about to be consumated.

Leaving nothing to chance, Bobby asked former President Eisenhower to lend his support. Congressmen and senators were also kept informed about the negotiations, most of whom approving what the government was doing. Only Senator Goldwater thought it was "demeaning" to offer bribes to Castro for the release of the prisoners.

With an image tarnished by the Kefauver Committee because of their price fixing practices, the drug manufacturers agreed to participate in the rescue mission, and thus redeem themselves. After a meeting with Dean Rusk, Douglas Dillon, Mortimer Caplin, and Stanley Surrey, the Government promised "tax advantages" to drug manufacturers who would cooperate.

At a lunch with Louis E. Oberfelder, the Assistant Attorney General in charge of the Department of Justice Tax Division, Bobby discussed the formula to get the project moving. The drug manufacturers, in doubt about public reaction, did not want to assume sole responsibility for the operation, afraid that some of the more reactionary members of Congress would accuse them of being soft on communism. For this reason, they wanted a government official to front for them.

On Monday, February 3, Warren Rogers Jr., in a *New York Herald Tribune* story, told the public for the first time that Bobby felt morally bound to help the Cuban prisoners.

While public opinion was being influenced to accept the plan, Castro suddenly developed temperamental attitudes. He told Donovan he would not release one prisoner until 20% of the drugs was first delivered in Havana. Donovan, of course, agreed.

Everyone was pleased; especially the drug manufacturers now seen as the great-hearted humanitarians motivated solely by a sincere desire to save human lives. The question of the special tax deduction was not raised.

Mitchell Rogovin, counsel to the Bureau of Internal Revenue Department, Surrey and Oberdorfer, and assisted by Lloyd Cutler, a Washington, D.C. lawyer, acting as the legal counselor for the Pharmaceutical Manufacturers Association, prepared the legal papers for the agreement, making sure that they would not have antitrust suits thrown at them. They were also told that it would not be necessary to disclose the actual costs of their products or give any markup data when filing for their tax reductions; in this way they would avoid exposing their price-fixing gimmicks. This windfall tax amounted to 52 % of the wholesale price of the product.

The American Red Cross, the semi-governmental charity organization, served as the distributing agency. Because of its prestige, the public would be more sympathetically disposed towards the project.

Bobby made numerous speeches on behalf of the Cubans. He spoke to the manufacturers of baby foods and drug corporation executives and described in detail the desperate plight of the Cubans who would surely die if not released.

Bobby's speeches, the tax deduction bait, and Mortimer Caplan's promise that tax deductions would be based on the value of the merchandise— which in turn would be based on the lowest wholesale catalogue price— were the magic ingredients that guaranteed the success of the negotiations.

The list of drugs and other products shipped to Havana took up 237 single-typed pages having more than 10,000 items. The first shipment was by plane to Florida on Friday, December 21.

The vast amount of red tape to expedite the movement of the material and clear the entry of the prisoners into the United States was unbelievable. Among the government departments involved in the program were the Civil Aeronautics Board, Interstate Commerce Commission, CIA, Air Force, Immigration and Naturalization Service, and the Department of Health, Education and Welfare. The Continental Insurance Company arranged for a $53,000,000 performance bond to be issued without any charge.

In Cuba, Donovan was told that the ransom money promised Castro on the release of the 60 prisoners had to be paid immediately. Nicholas Katzenbach of the Justice Department petitioned to get the Royal Bank of Canada to issue a Letter of Credit. It was the Morgan Guaranty Trust Company and Bank of America that finally came to the rescue.

On leaving Washington for Miami, Donovan suddenly dropped out of sight. The CIA had him taken to a hideaway to confer with Castro by telephone. After two days of telephone negotiations, he left for Havana.

Three Cuban Red Cross officials dressed in olive tinted uniforms, all heavy-bearded and smoking huge black cigars, arrived in Florida for an inspection of the material. Satisfied that all was in order, they returned to Havana on December 23.

Bobby was now reasonably certain that the prisoners would soon be out of Cuba. Enrique Ruiz Williams, on learning that Bobby was trying to reach him, phoned from a pay station, managing to contact him at his home in McLean, Virginia.

"You got it, Enrique," Bobby jubilantly exclaimed. "This is it. The guy with the beard has accepted."

Yet, there was another snag. Castro had released the first batch of prisoners to the African Pilot docked in Havana. Then another planeload. By 6:05 PM on December 23, a total of 426 men had been released. In Washington everyone was elated except for Donovan. He knew that the remainder of the prisoners would not be turned loose until the $2,900,000 was paid.

Bobby phoned Cardinal Cushing and got a pledge for $1 million dollars. He then called General Lucius Clay and got the balance of $1,900,000. Clay in turn contacted Robert B. Anderson and Robert Knight and had them get Texaco, the Standard Oil Company of New Jersey, and the Ford Motor Company to underwrite the loan. On being told that a Letter of Credit covering the full amount was on deposit in the Royal Bank of Canada, Castro released the prisoners. By 9:55 PM all of the Cuban prisoners had landed in Miami. Bobby felt proud of his accomplishment, also because an additional 30 Americans (three of whom were CIA agents) were released from Cuban jails. All in all some 10,000 Cubans gained their freedom as a result of those extensive negotiations.

Chapter 20
Plotting the Assassination

The Cuban adventure was not to end with the Bay of Pigs fiasco. During the early part of November 1961, the New York Times' Latin American correspondent, Tad Szulc, was asked by his good friend, Richard Goodwin, special assistant to the President, to go to the Department of Justice for a talk with Attorney General Kennedy. That off-the-record meeting took place on November 8. The two men discussed ways and means to dispose of Castro. The Administration had suffered a humiliating defeat and both the Chief Executive and Attorney General, conditioned as it were by Father Joe, were not taking it gracefully. After a lengthy talk with Bobby, Szulc conferred with President Kennedy for over an hour.

On being asked by the President the ramifications of a Castro assassination, Szulc said that such an act would not necessarily cause the Cuban system to collapse, making it quite evident that he found the suggestion shocking.

"I agree with you completely," President Kennedy said. Then he stressed the fact that both he and his brother believed that the country, for purely moral reasons, should never be in a situation where the only recourse would be to kill a foreign leader not to our liking. At that point President Kennedy said he had broached the question because he was curious to learn the reporter's reactions. In passing, he complained about the tremendous pressure exerted by a number of advisors determined to have Castro assassinated. While the President and his brother told newspapermen that murdering foreign leaders was not in their plans, it did not deter from finding other ways to eliminate Castro.

Sometime in November 1962, a major covert action aimed at getting rid of Castro was being formulated. Richard Goodwin and General Edward Landsdale, an old hand in the game of counter- insurgency, in close cooperation with Bobby played important roles in conceiving and developing the project known as "Operation Mongoose." Goodwin told the President that Bobby "would be a most effective commander of the operation." In a special memorandum addressed to the Attorney General, Goodwin mentioned the basic points of the impending plan. Landsdale said that, "a picture has emerged clearly enough to indicate what needs to be done and to support your sense of urgency concerning Cuba."

Towards the end of the month, President Kennedy issued a memorandum in which he urged the "use of our available assets to help overthrow the Communist regime."

Shortly afterwards a newly-formed group— the Special Group (augmented) SGA— was set up to plan and oversee the actions. Included in that contingent were McGeorge Bundy; Alexis Johnson, State Department functionary; Roswell Gilpatric, Department of Defense; John McCone; General Lyman Lemnitzer, Joint Chief of Staff; Attorney General Kennedy; General Maxwell Taylor; Secretary of State Dean Rusk; and Secretary of Defense Robert McNamara. General Landsdale was assigned as director of the operation. Goodwin, however, wanted Bobby, but the President did not agree. Instead, General Taylor was appointed to serve as chairman of the Special Group and Bobby assumed an active role in day-by-day activities. It was emphasized that the role by the Attorney General be completely "unrelated" to his duties as the nation's chief law officer.

During the latter part of 1962, William Harvey was appointed the director of the CIA's Task Force W, its unit in Mongoose. That force was to operate in conjunction with Special Group (augmented) and included a staff of 400 agents working out of the CIA headquarters and its Miami station. Both McCone and Harvey were in charge of Mongoose. Although Helms, the CIA chieftain, was present at 17 out of the 40 Mongoose meetings, he was considered very much a part of the project.

During the fall of 1961, the President told the overly- zealous General Landsdale to brief himself on the Administration's Cuban policies and to come up with some sound recommendations. As a result, Landsdale was forced to concede that Castro had been able to gain "considerable affection for himself from the people of Cuba," and suggested that the United States "should take a very different course": Instead of the "harassment" operations, utilize those Cubans who had opposed Batista and who had differences with Castro, to help upset that government. The plan called for involving prominent professionals in establishing fronts against the bearded leader and creating "cells and activities inside Cuba that could work secretly and safely."

While all those discussions were going on, Bissell, another CIA chieftain, was invited to come to the White House where, to his chagrin, the two brothers "chewed him out" for "sitting on his ass and not doing anything about getting rid of the Castro regime."

On January 19, 1962, a meeting of key activists was held in the offices of the Attorney General. Present were: General Landsdale, McManus, General Craig (representing the Joint Chiefs of Staff), Don Wilson of USIA, Major Patchell of McNamara's office, and Frank Hand of the CIA. Mr. Hand, Helm's Executive Assistant, recorded the following statement made by Bobby:

"... a solution to the Cuban problem today carries top priority in the United States government — no time, money, effort or manpower is to be spared."

Helms later said that with "that kind of atmosphere," he surmised that the idea of assassination was very definitely in the minds of Robert Kennedy and the others. McManus agreed with that perception, adding that the Attorney General "was very vehement in his speech" and "really wanted action," but that "it never occured to me" that the Kennedy exhortation was meant to countenance murder as a weapon to dispatch Castro.

Landsdale began his actions on January 18, 1962. He enlightened the participating agencies about the 32 planning tasks that ranged from intelligence collections to planning the "use" of the United States military forces to support an internal Cuban uprising. It also called for the sabotaging of many economic enterprises on the island.

Fully realizing those plans needed to be cleared with the Attorney General, Lansdale submitted a copy on January 18, 1962 with a handwritten note: "My review does not include the sensitive work reported to you. I felt you preferred informing the President privately." Later on, when Landsdale testified before the Church committee, he suddenly had a lapse of memory, saying that the "sensitive work" referred to had nothing to do with the subject murder, but that he may have been referring to a trip he had made to Florida to assess the political potency of the Cubans.

In another memorandum sent to Bobby Kennedy, Landsdale said: "We might uncork the touchdown play independently of the institutional program we are spurring." What did he mean? Was it a fanciful way of telling the Attorney General that the plan to kill Castro was now in progress? Or, as he explained, "Just a breezy way of referring to the Cuban uprising that was being encouraged by the Kennedy Administration?"

Landsdale proved very capable in dredging up novel ways to wreck the Cuban government. Parrott, one of his close associates, with just a hint of sarcasm, said that one such suggestion would have the flamboyant Cecil B. DeMille groan with envy:

"I'll give you one example of Landsdale's perspicacity. He had a wonderful plan for getting rid of Castro. This plan called for spreading the word that the Second Coming of Christ was imminent and that Christ was against Castro who was anti-Christ. And you would spread the word around Cuba, and then, on whatever date it was, there would be a manifestation of this thing. And at that time, (this is absolutely true), and at that time, just over the horizon there would be an American submarine which would surface off Cuba and send up some starshells. This would be the manifestation of the Second Coming and Castro would be overthrown."

A far more dangerous suggestion conjured up by Landsdale called for the incapacitation of Cuban sugar workers during harvest time by the use of chemical warfare. Landsdale explained that certain chemicals would sicken the workers temporarily and keep them away from the fields for 24 to 48 hours. The higher authorities, however, did approve the use of "gangster elements" that "might provide the best recruitment potential for actions against the police and Intelligence Agents." In an earlier report about the use of "gangster elements" (January 24, 1962), those law-abiding citizens were mentioned in a CIA memorandum for the SGA.

Commenting on Task 5, Landsdale's unit, calling for the defection of important Cuban government officials, the memorandum included a special note: Planning for the task at hand will "necessarily be based upon an appeal made inside the island by intermediaries," and listed "crime syndicates," along with others, as possible "intermediaries."

Another Landsdale brainstorm which he discussed with Bobby could have been called a Caribbean version of a Wild West bounty hunter's escapade. "Operation Bounty" was described as a "system of financial rewards commensurate with the position and stature for killing, or delivering alive, known Communists." It called for the dropping of flyers over Cuba offering rewards of $5,000 for the heads of minor officials and up to $100,000 for key government leaders. Landsdale thought it was a piece of Machiavellian cunning. He offered two cents for the head of Castro, later explaining that the sum of two cents was meant to "denigrate him in the eyes of his fellow countrymen." This brilliant suggestion was also filed away and forgotten by the Attorney General.

Ever since Operation Mongoose of November 30, 1961, both Kennedys were fully cognizant of these activities and those of other agencies. The President said that SGA should be kept "closely informed of all its activities," an assistant of William Harvey's later testified, including every "nauseating" detail.

Bobby was always telling his cohorts that the President was not pleased with the progress being achieved, and "stressed that Mongoose had been underway for a year and that there had been as yet no serious acts of sabotage, and that one major effort had failed twice."

Serving as chairman at Group meetings, on October 16, Bobby said that he was going to give Mongoose more personal attention in view of the lack of progress, that he would conduct daily meetings with Landsdale, Harvey, and the other agency people.

While the word "assassination" was never mentioned by the highest authorities, Helms, who directed covert operations (when poison pills had been handed to gangster Rosselli in Miami during April 1962 to be used to kill Castro), later testified that "those of us who were still [in the Agency] were enormously anxious to try and be successful at what we were being asked to do by what was then a relatively new Administration. We wanted to earn our spurs with the President and other officers of the Kennedy Administration."

He also said that intense pressure exerted by the Kennedy Administration to overthrow Castro had led him to perceive that the CIA was acting within the scope of its authority in attempting to kill the Cuban head of government even though the word assassination had never been mentioned:

"I believe it was the policy at the time to get rid of Castro and if killing him was one of the things that was to be done in this connection, that was within what was expected."

Later, at one point during a Senate (Church) Committee hearing on the Cuban situation, Senator Mathias drew an example from history for Helms:

"When Thomas a. Beckett was proving an annoyance, as Castro, the King said 'who will rid me of this man?' He didn't say to somebody, 'go out and murder him.' He said, 'who will rid me of this man?' and let it go at that."

"That is a warning reference to the problem," Helms replied.

"You feel that spans the generations and the centuries?" Mathias asked.

"I think it does, Sir," Helms answered.

An official in the Western Hemisphere Division of the Directorate of Plans, responsible for evaluating potential Cuban assets, testified that in June or July 1962 he was told by his chief (either Harvey or his assistant) "to go see the Attorney General. He has something to talk about."

Robert Kennedy instructed him "to see a man who has contact with a small group of Cubans who have a plan for creating an insurrection or something like that."

There were five to six Cubans who, claiming connections on the island, asked for weapons to start an insurrection. On being told that the Cubans had no concrete plan, Bobby rejected the official's evaluation and ordered him to go to the Guantanamo Naval Base and to use "whatever assets we could get to make contact with people inside Cuba and start working and developing this particular group." When the official protested and said that the CIA had decided not to operate out of the base, Kennedy replied, "We'll see about that."

On being asked by the Church Committee if Robert Kennedy had ever told him to order the murder of Castro, Helms came out with a straight "no."

"He did not?" the Chairman asked.

"Not in those words, no," Helms answered.

Senator Huddlestom asked Helms whether "it did not occur to you to inquire of the Attorney General or the Special Group or of anyone else that when they kept pushing and asking for action— to clarify that question of whether you should actually be trying to assassinate?"

"I don't know whether it was in training, experience, tradition or exactly what one points to, but I think to go to a Cabinet officer and say am I right in assuming that you want to assassinate Castro or to try to assassinate Castro is a question it wouldn't have occurred to me to ask."

Dean Rusk, Ross Gilpatrick, Bundy and the other government officials before the Church Committee said that the President and Attorney General were constantly urging the Task Force to "knock off" Castro, but none indicated that they wanted him murdered. To "knock off" was interpreted to mean that the Castro Regime was to be destroyed. In his testimony, however, Robert McNamara brought to the fore embarrassing contradictions suggesting that those men were involved in the more unseemly aspect of Operation Mongoose.

The Chairman referring to McNamara: "We have received evidence from your senior associates that they never participated in the authorization of an assassination attempt against Castro nor ever directed the CIA to undertake such   attempts.

"We have testimony establishing the chain of command where covert action was concerned, and all of it has been to the effect that the Special Group or the Special Group (Augmented) had full charge of covert operations, and that in that chain of command any proposals to do with Castro personally were to be laid before the Special Group (Augmented) and were not to be undertaken except with the authority of that Group and at the direction of that Group.

"Now at the same time we know from the evidence that the CIA was in fact engaged during the period in a series of attempts to assassinate Castro. Now you know where we are faced with this dilemma. Either the CIA was a rogue elephant rampaging out of control over which no effective direction was being given in this matter of assassination, or there was some secret channel circumventing the whole structure of command by which the CIA and certain officials in the CIA were authorized to proceed with the assassination plots, assassination attempts against Castro. In the third and final point that I can think of is that somehow these officials of the CIA who were so engaged misunderstood or misinterpreted their scope of activity and authority."

McNamara had the following statement to make to the Committee: "I can only tell you what will further your uneasiness. Because I have stated before and I believe today that the CIA was a highly disciplined organization fully under the control of the government I must assume responsibility for the actions of the two, putting assassination aside for the moment. But I know of no major action taken by the CIA during the time I was in the government that it was not properly authorized by senior officials. And when I say that I want to emphasize also that I believe with hindsight we authorized actions that were contrary to the interests of the republic but I don't want it on the record that the CIA was uncontrolled, was operating with its own authority and we can be absolved of responsibility for what the CIA did again with exception of assassination again, which I say I never heard of...

"I find it almost inconceivable that the assassination attempts were carried out during the Kennedy Administration without senior members knowing it and I understand the contradictions that this carries with respect to the facts."

At a meeting held August 10, 1962, Landsdale told Harvey to include as part of Phase II Mongoose, an option for the liquidation of leaders. Inspector General Harris stated that "the subject of a Castro assassination was raised at the meeting at State on August 10, 1962, but it was unrelated to any actual attempts at assassination. It did result in the Mongoose action memorandum by Landsdale assigning to the CIA plan for the liquidation of leaders."

In brief, neither Bobby Kennedy nor the President, members of his cabinet nor the CIA actually had the word *assassination* mentioned on any of the documents, but the subject was always brought up at the meetings of the Special Group (Augmented), in the Oval Office and, of course, at the Justice Department.

Citing the example of King Henry II giving veiled hints to his courtiers to rid him of Thomas a. Beckett when he questioned Helms was in a sense accusing the Kennedy brothers of doing the same thing.

And the fact remains that whereas Beckett was actually murdered, Castro today is more than just stroking his graying beard.

Chapter 21

Homelife with Ethel and the Children

Bobby was fortunate to have a home to go to where he could relax with his children and with Ethel, who, by temperament if not by birth, was a typical Kennedy, dedicated to her husband and children.

A slim, brown-haired woman with a cheerful disposition, she always showed strong maternal instincts. While she could easily afford nurses and governesses, she saw to it that her offspring received the proper upbringing and education.

Bobby and Ethel first met— he was 19 and she only 17— while on a ski trip with Eunice, Pat and Jean to Mount Tremblant in Quebec. Later, Ethel recalled that Bobby appeared unable to make up his mind whether he preferred her sister, Pat, or her:

"He took me out for two weeks; then he started taking out my sister Pat. Pat is three years older than I am and much prettier and more intellectual."

Bobby, like the other Kennedy men, was a detached rather than an impulsive kind of lover. He paid court for five-and-a-half years before proposing marriage which finally took place in Greenwich, Connecticut; his brother John was their best man.

Ethel faced no problem adjusting to a Kennedy way of life. She liked to participate in sports and was good at most games, especially at touch football. Her love of life and her exhuberance helped her in every conceivable type of situation. When a cheer leader at Waseda University in Tokyo accidentally hit her in the stomach, Ethel laughed it off, although she had been hurt and was in pain.

She worked long hours in all of John F. Kennedy's campaigns as well as those of her husband, licking stamps, sealing envelopes, entertaining at all the social teas, and voicing her opinions on many different issues.

During the 1952 campaign when John was running against Senator Henry Cabot Lodge, Ethel made courtesy calls to hundreds of housewives, cajoling them into voting for her brother-in-law. At the many political meetings, she was truly the stellar attraction.

As the late President said, Ethel, together with the other Kennedy women, "drowned Senator Lodge in 700 gallons of tea," and thus retired him permanently from the Senate.

Ethel was also active in the West Virginia and Wisconsin primaries. The novelist James Michner was tremendously impressed with Ethel, stating that she was "one of the most politically sophisticated women [he] had ever met."

The editors of *Life Magazine* praised Bobby's magic among the natives while on a trip to the Ivory Coast. But the writers who covered the trip thought that Ethel was a very effective spokeswoman on the American way of life. She journeyed to many villages, making friends with local leaders. On discovering a *Prefect* with ten children, she admitted to being jealous, as he was three up on her. The African official naturally liked her wit, later admitting that he was impressed by her.

On learning that Bobby intended to take her along on a trip to the French colonies, she bought records and practiced French with Jackie. In Rome, a local boy dared her to ride on his motor scooter. She boarded the vehicle and sped through the heavy traffic, colliding with a small car, but escaping with minor injuries. On a visit to Queen Juliana of The Netherlands, a house servant accidentally closed a car door on her foot. Ethel, naturally, took it in stride.

Bobby was also the type of individual who rose to a challenge. While driving through Sun Valley, Idaho, he unexpectedly saw a difficult ski slide a short distance away. He got out of the car, put on his skiis, and in no time was whizzing down—hill at neck-breaking speed.

The couple worked and played hard, instilling their sense of ethics and deep feelings in their children. Bobby's discipline, however, was much milder toward the children than was his father's: "We try to give the older children the [kind of] punishment that will benefit them and enrich their lives, like being sent to their rooms to read. Sometimes we deprive them of something they like. They also get spanked."

The children enjoyed their father's presence. Bobby always had dinner with them at least three times a week. He also spent a few hours in the afternoon playing games with them.

Both Ethel and Bobby shared a dislike for night clubs, preferring to give small dinner parties at home where Bobby would receive the guests. He usually wore slacks and a sweater, and liked to sprawl on a sofa or on the floor. Ethel, meanwhile, tended the bar. She made excellent daiquiries, using chopped lime peels and a thick coating of sugar around the rims of the glasses— her favorite drink.

The house cook almost always prepared the meals, usually lap dinners, for Bobby's taste was quite simple: thick lamb chops, lyonnaise potatoes, green salad, desert, chocolate souffle, and ice cream with chocolate sauce.

If guests were in the house, the children would go to bed as soon as they got the signal to do so. Ethel and Bobby excused themselves to go upstairs to listen to them say their prayers, to recite one decade of the rosary, and to read at least two chapters from the Bible. If the parents were out, the two older children supervised the nightly prayers.

One could easily see that Ethel and Bobby were very religious. Neither questioned the dogma of their church. Gore Vidal (when he was their intimate friend), related the following incident:

Bobby had organized a weekly seminar for junior government people, having invited historians, economists, political scientists and philosophers together with wives. A.W. Ayer of the University of London lectured on philosophy. Towards the end, Eunice leaned over towards Ethel and whispered, "I don't think the professor believes in God." As Ayer was about to conclude, Ethel asked him to explain his rejection of metaphysics. Puzzled, Ayer asked, "What do you mean by metaphysics?" Bobby, seeing his wife getting into hot water, told her to "can it!" Undaunted, Ethel continued: "I mean whether conceptions like truth, virtue and beauty have any meaning?" Although there is no record of Ayer's reply, Vidal didn't think Ethel really knew what Ayer was talking about.

She lacked one talent: she simply could not cook. "I never did very well at cooking. Once I tried to fix an omelet. I called my sister in Connecticut and asked her how to cook it. She started to tell me, beginning with the breaking of the eggs but I said, no, I mean what do you do after it has already fallen?"

Bobby was not a very demonstrative man. At a dinner sponsored by the Women's National Press Club in Washington, Bobby, detained at the Justice Department, arrived late. Ethel rushed to his side to kiss him. Noticing the photographers nearby, he held her off at arms length. Ethel's face turned a beet red. Jackie, noticing her sister-in-law's discomfiture, walked over and embraced her. Lyndon Baines Johnson, the *kissingest* politician in Washington, also saw what had happened. He pranced over to Ethel's side and implanted a large loud kiss on her red cheeks.

Ethel and Bobby preferred light entertainment, unlike Jackie, who visited art museums, went to concerts, professional football games, to light movies and plays. Bobby liked animals. With Ethel, who also found them delightful, they often went to Hickory Hill, a small zoo which had a number of parakeets, several over-sized canines, horses, ponies, ducks, geese, goats and a varied assortment of wild life.

The couple owned a seal lion. A very playful animal, it loved to swim in the family pool and to chase the guests all over the lawn. One day, the seal flipped its way down to the McLean food market where he chased the customers out of the store, causing a quasi-comical pandemonium. Pursuant to this escapade, Bobby took the seal to the Washington Zoo for a new, permanent residence.

Ethel thought Robert was the perfect husband, except for one thing: his dancing. "[It] is a joke!"

At a party to celebrate their 12th wedding anniversary, Ethel was sitting at a table far out on a bridge thrown across the pool. When Arthur Schlesinger Jr. and his dancing partner walked on the bridge, it trembled under the additional weight. On seeing Ethel's chair sag, Schlesinger looked on with horror, trying to warn Ethel what was about to happen. Engrossed in a conversation, she did not realize the danger. Suddenly, Ethel fell over the side and into the water. Schlesinger, fully clothed, plunged in and helped her out. Though drenched, Ethel was not a bit put out. She began to laugh, and in no time, had all of the guests laughing with her

One problem prevented Ethel and Bobby from having a normal life— an army of photographers pursuing them all over the place.

While vacationing in Hyannis Port, Robert Jr. had broken his arm and was wearing a cast. Courtney, on the other hand, had a cast on her leg from a previous injury. Bobby had given explicit instructions to the Secret Service agents not to let any photographers get inside the compound. A few weeks later, a major publication published pictures of the children in their casts. Furious, Bobby accused the agents of allowing the photographers to take the pictures. They swore that they did not allow any photographer inside the place. They did not know that ace photographer Stan Tretick had been teaching Schlesinger's 12-year old son to use a camera. Later, they discovered that Stan had helped Mark set up the children for the pictures.

With the assassination of John, Bobby and Ethel took in Caroline and John-John. A former governess said there was no doubt that Bobby represented a father image to the orphaned children.

One afternoon when Caroline was walking down Fifth Avenue, she saw her uncle approaching. "There's Bob!" she exclaimed, as she ran towards him. She then jumped into his arms just as she used to do with her father.

Chapter 22

Journeys to Far-away Places

In 1947, Bobby went to the Middle East as an accredited correspondent for International News Service. On seeing the seven Arab armies invade Palestine, he predicted that the Israelis, because of their superior morale, would defeat them.

In 1955, he traveled to Teheran where he met with Supreme Court Justice William O. Douglas. The two met with the Shah, who revealed that he was the landlord of 200 villages on the shores of the Caspian Sea and that he had long decided to divide the land among the peasants. Although the Shah eventually got around to divide his land holdings, the other Iranian aristocrats never did.

On their Russian tour, they found the citizens in the provinces to be better dressed and better mannered than those in Moscow. Abandoned by their guide in Baku, Bobby and the Justice, suspecting that their room was bugged, suggested out loud to put a call through to Khrushchev in Moscow. A few minutes later, a Russian official appeared to tell the two Americans that a new guide had been assigned to show them around. The guide got them seats on the trains and special rooms at hotels, as well as front row seats at the theaters; surely *red* carpet treatment all the way.

Although Bobby ate lamb's ear, lamb's brain, head of lamb and watermelon by the car load, he did not find Russian food very appetizing. He started the trip weighing 160 pounds. Three months later he was down to 143. While the natives were friendly, the officials were a different breed, very aloof toward the ordinary citizens. Some Russians spoke about the execution of Sacco and Vanzetti in Massachusetts. They thought the two Italo-American anarchists were innocent and believed that their execution was tantamount to legal murder. Douglas told the indignant Russians that the accused had been found guilty, but it did not turn the natives' sympathy. During the discourse, Bobby did not say anything about the executions; perhaps he had heard about the two men in Russia for the first time.

On his next trip, he went with his brother—then Congressman John Kennedy—and their sister Pat to Japan, India, Thailand, Malaysia, Indo-China, and Pakistan where they met Prime Minister Liaquat Ai Khan who, three days later, was assassinated. In Kuala Lumpar, they rode in a tank through guerrilla infested areas. In Tokyo, they met Dr. Gunji Hosono, the Director of the Japan Institute of Foreign Affairs. He and Joseph Kennedy had met when Joe was U.S. Ambassador at the Court of St. James. Dr.Mosono urged Bobby to make another trip to Japan to ease the bitterness evident among Japanese college students towards America.

In 1961, after a stop-over in Japan, Bobby went to troubled Indonesia where Sukarno had laid claim to West New Guinea while the Dutch held fast to the territory. The Communist bloc promised to send large arm shipments to Sukarno. Bobby arrived in Jakarta just as things had turned for the worse. In his book, *Just Friends and Friendly Enemies,* Bobby wrote that the United States was being charged with giving "at least token backing to an internal revolutionary force that had tried to overthrow the Sukarno regime." Nevertheless, he was treated politely.

Carlos Romulo of the Philippines, an ardent admirer of American culture, told Bobby that the struggle against communism would never be won until the United States resolved its "Negro problem."

Japanese businessmen wanted to know when the United States would get out of Okinawa, and worried about the possibility of increased tariffs on their exports to the United States. Socialist party leaders discussed the suspension of all atom bomb testing, suggesting the great powers establish a free nuclear zone in the Pacific. Bobby believed a system was imperative for inspection and control before an agreement could be reached with Russia. He also told the Socialists that the United States had offered to ban the bomb one at a time, but that the Russians did not want the Americans to inspect their atomic reactors and launching sites. At Waseda University, a group of students shouted him down. On discovering the microphone had gone dead because the electricity had been turned off, he called it a day and left. The Socialists told Bobby that the United States was a lair for "monopoly capitalists," and he suggested that they read some modern books on the American economy. He told a group of lawyers that Japan had made a remarkable recovery since the end of World War II. When one expressed his appreciation for the flattery, Bobby startled them with this rejoinder: "This is a helluva long way to come just to flatter somebody. I can do that back home." When a Buddhist priest gave him some incense sticks to burn, he turned to U.S. Ambassador Edwin O. Reischaur: "What are the implications if I do this?"

"It just shows respect," the Ambassador answered.

"You're sure it won't look as if I'm worshipping Buddha?"

In Indonesia, while speaking before 2000 law students and faculty, a young man threw a hardshell fruit at him, striking Bobby on the nose. Undaunted, he fielded many questions, ranging from the American-Mexican War to Roman and German history. At a reception given by Attorney General Gunawan, Ethel danced the "Twist" with Grandon Groven, a State Department official. Bobby remarked that the writer's terpsichorean talents were brilliant, but that Groven's "Twist" was like a "dehydrated Charleston."

In West Berlin, over 180,000 people waited in the cold to see him. He called The Wall "a snake across the heart of the city." Praising the West Berliners for their courage in standing up to the Russians, he said that The Wall had been erected by Walter Ulbricht because he could not "tolerate the contrast between freedom and communism." He also told the crowd that if Berlin were invaded by Russian or East German troops, the U.S. would regard it as if Chicago, New York, London or Paris were being attacked. Finally, in an emotional outburst, he cried out, "You are our brothers and we stand by you." He visited the Ploetzenses, the prison where German Army officers were executed for the attempted assassination of Hitler, placing a wreath as a token of respect for the murdered men. Mrs. Julius Leber, the widow of the Socialist leader who had participated in the plot to kill Hitler, told Bobby that Americans should learn that there were Germans who had opposed the Nazi dictatorship. In Bonn, he spoke before the West German Society of Foreign Affairs whose membership included leading businessmen,financiers,economists and intellectuals. He told them that Americans viewed the development of the European Common Market with a great deal of sympathy, predicting that De Gaulle would not slam the door in the face of the British. After a brief outline of American history, he praised the Germans for contributing $1.4 billion in foreign aid to the underdeveloped nations, and suggested that they should continue to support that program.

In Paris, he spoke for about 45 minutes with Charles De Gaulle on world problems.

Bobby's trips drew a lot of criticism. Mayor John V. Lindsay, who had fought Bobby when he attempted to get his wire-tap bill passed, asked "whether this kind of Madison Avenue approach is the stuff of which foreign policy is made."

Bobby accomplished no tangible results. Sukarno's Indonesia waged war against Malaysia, West Germany still entertained hopes of snatching territory lost to Poland, De Gaulle was still intent on kicking the Americans out of Europe and keeping Great Britain out of the Common Market, and the Iron Curtain was still shut down tight. Nevertheless, Bobby made one gain: he had become an expert on foreign policy.

Chapter 23

Bobby and his Vice Presidency Nomination

With the Democratic Party's national convention two months off, Bobby, still feeling the impact of his brother's assassination, realized he could not be Attorney General for much longer. His supporters put out feelers to learn if the big bosses in New York State would support him as a candidate for the U.S. Senate, and were encouraged by their responses. Earlier, a few misguided friends had attempted to corral delegates in New Hampshire in support of Bobby as a Vice Presidential nominee, making Lyndon Johnson furious. It was natural for Johnson to suspect Bobby. When Johnson learned that it was Paul Corbin who had instigated the move, the President had him fired. Later Bobby offered to make a public announcement disclaiming any intention on his part to seek the nomination, and told his enthusiastic partisans to stop their activities.

If some were convinced he had no ambitions for that nomination, others became confused after he delivered a speech to the students at the District of Columbia High School where he stated that he was "not going to remain as Attorney General after November. Right now, I'm only interested in finishing up as Attorney General. I may go back to Massachusetts or elsewhere."

Just what did he mean by "elsewhere?" In truth, he wanted to be the second banana on the national ticket. When Governor Michael DeSalle, a Kennedy admirer, said that Bobby would make an excellent Vice President, Johnson again became increasingly annoyed, accusing Bobby that he was trying to force his hand.

In New York, Bobby's supporters were waiting to learn his decision as they could get him the nomination to run for the Senate. But Bobby still nourished the idea to run for Vice President. He showed his hand after his brother, Ted, was almost killed in an airplane crash. Encouraged by his trusted advisors, he said to a few key people that Johnson did not want him on his ticket, thus making it clear that he would accept an offer from Johnson.

Meanwhile, Bobby continued to speak before high school students, university legal groups and juvenile delinquency organizations, trying to create a groundswell of public support to get Johnson to choose him. In a speech at Marquette University, he even imitated his older brother's brand of humor:

"Years ago, I was a hard-working lawyer making $4,200 a year. I took my work home every night and was very diligent. Ten years later I became Attorney General of the United States. So, you see, if you want to become successful just get your brother elected President."

Now on his own, he told a reporter that his "main interest [was] to remain in government service and continue the things we started." A few weeks later however, he said he would like to get away from Washington altogether.

Many important men in the Johnson camp, nevertheless, wanted Bobby to remain in public life. One said that Bobby "is one of the half-dozen men in the country today qualified for top political leadership." Another expressed his gratification for the fact that he "was coming back into his own and behaving like the old Bobby Kennedy, " further observing that he "presses a little less, but he's gotten back the old shattering candor which can be so frightening and so useful."

Bobby asked Johnson to send him to Vietnam as Ambassador. But Johnson, told him that he did not want the responsibility of endangering his health and his life in the strife-torn South Vietnam. Instead, Johnson contemplated sending Bobby to Indonesia where Sukarno's soldiers had been infiltrating into North Borneo.

Johnson saw the occasion to get Bobby out of Washington. He told his cronies that the boy seemed to find Sukarno simpatico. Why not have him talk with the Indonesian leader, President Macapagal of the Philippines and Tunku Abdul Rahman, Malaysia's chief of state. Why not indeed!

When the independently-minded Prince Sihanouk learned of the meeting, he tried to participate but was turned down by Bobby. His feelings bruised, the Prince said that Bobby's remarks were "a model of insolence and hostility presented under a veneer of politeness."

The meeting appeared successful. Sukarno promised to stop the fighting, and the other rulers spoke about permanent peace in Southeast Asia. On leaving, Bobby felt confident that peace would return to that part of the world. However, he soon learned otherwise. On his way to London, he was told that a mob of 15,000 was demonstrating in Jakarta, while Sukarno was telling his countrymen to "go onward, never retreat... crush

118

Malaysia."

In London, Bobby met Duncan Sandys and Rab Butler, the British Foreign Secretary. Bobby spoke with Sandys in a gruff way. Taking offense, Butler told Bobby that he had no right to talk to a member of the British Cabinet in that way. Bobby reiterated that he never minced words whenever he had anything to say. On realizing that he may have gone too far, Bobby smiled and said, "Mr. Sandys, you're as popular in the East as I am in Alabama."

When he returned to Washington, Johnson told him that he had carried out "his assignment constructively and with real achievement." A few weeks later, however, fighting began again in the jungles of North Borneo. Bobby, who had some of his brother's talent for self-deprecation, remarked: "So nothing has been lost but two weeks of shooting and killing."

Back at Hickory Hill, Bobby occupied himself with his family which now included Caroline and John-John, and Jackie, who took her two children to Bobby's house every day.

"They think of it as their home," Jackie said. "Anything that comes up involving a father, like father's day at school, I always mention Bobby's name. Caroline shows him her report cards. She makes drawings at school marked 'To Uncle Bobby.'

"We used to think that if anything happened to us we'd want to leave the children with Ethel and Bobby. But we always felt they had their own big responsibilities. Now I want them to be a part of that family. Bobby wants to look after his brother's children. There's John, with his brother's name. He's going to make sure John turns out as he should."

Bobby's solicitude for his brother's family was not confined to the the children. When Jackie left the White House and bought a home in Georgetown, Bobby helped her set the place in order. He also took her along on a vacation in Antigua, urging her to play tennis and suggesting that she take up skiing.

The pain was still there, especially in seeing the White House occupied by a President who bore him no good will. Bobby felt deep rancor on hearing comments to the effect that the country's foreign policy decisions would not now "be made from a rocking chair"— obvious allusion to his brother's back injury.

A newspaperman once asked him what pained him the most about the present.

"Just the fact that *he's* not here."

An intimate friend wanted to know why he bothered with politics when he could stay home and enjoy life with his family. Bobby conceded that he was fortunate in his family but could not see himself wasting his days away as a country squire. He was, after all, a product of his father's teachings, and Joe Kennedy had always insisted that his children have a definite goal in life.

Bobby's aim now was the Vice Presidency. Lyndon Johnson, who was 56 years old, had already suffered a massive heart attack. The actuarial tables for a man with that kind of medical history are not good. Bobby could not help but be aware of the fact that Johnson, who always worked under pressure, could fall victim to another attack.

Was it possible to set things in motion and get Johnson to accept him as Vice President? Johnson was aware that Bobby's name was being projected all over the nation, that the Kennedy Memorial Library was "the intellectual branch of the Kennedy Party," and that Ted Kennedy was touring the Western states on a speaking marathon, attracting huge audiences.

On a trip to Poland, with Ethel and three of their children, Bobby kept the American Embassy staff in a state of high tension. He visited several historical sites, and held many discussions with Polish government officials.

Washington had recognized the fact that Poland had no choice but to maintain good relations with the Soviet Union, that nothing must be done in Warsaw to arouse the suspicions of the Kremlin, believing that Poland represented a "liberal outpost" within the Eastern Bloc.

At the American Embassy, a crowd of over 1,000 men, women and children waited to greet him. Climbing on top of his automobile with Ethel, he told the Poles that his "brother would not have been elected if it weren't for the Polish vote back home." Finding the top of a car convenient, he went on making other speeches in the same way. He visited Cardinal Wyszinski and accused the government officials for evading their responsibilities to create a more peaceful world." He thought it wise for the Poles to change their policy towards West Germany, urging the Warsaw Government to encourage the East Germans to become part of a unified Germany. Wladyslaw Gomulka told Bobby to see Auschweitz— the Nazi death camp— where millions of Jews and other nationals had been murdered. The Polish premier believed it would help give him a better understanding of his government's feelings towards Germany. But Bobby never got around to it.

In Bonn, he called for the reunification of Germany.

Johnson was unimpressed. He would not have him as Vice President regardless of what Bobby said. Not a month after Dallas, Johnson had already told Kenneth O'Donnel that he would "never have a Kennedy on the ticket."

Bobby entertained a hope that Johnson might change his mind, thinking that a documentary on his brother would stampede the delegates into voting for him at the national convention. On learning that the film had been scheduled to be shown at the beginning of the convention, with Jackie Kennedy expected to make an appearance, the wily Johnson ordered it be screened at the end of the convention. Jackie got the hint and went to Atlantic City, only to appear at the John R. Kennedy exhibit outside the hall.

Bobby should have spared himself the effort to persuade Johnson from the start, knowing that from the power base of the Vice Presidency, he would have presented a clear and present danger for the Texan. As it turned out, Bobby was lucky not to have gotten himself nominated.

Johnson spread the word that Sargent Shriver was being considered as a candidate. Shriver, they said, was a natural— a Kennedy of sorts by marriage, and the driving force behind the Peace Corps. He was a Roman Catholic to boot— a perfect combination, bound to please everyone, including Bobby. But the perfect choice quickly became an imperfect one. A loyal member of the Kennedy clan, Shriver would never usurp the place that rightfully belonged to Bobby. Besides, he had no political base. Even Mayor Daley, the Democratic boss in Chicago, couldn't see Shriver for dust— so said Johnson's men.

Rumors spread that Robert McNamara was being chosen. This modern Thor, who had displayed such talents as the chief administrator over the immense Defense establishment, would go down well with the major industrialists. He was reputed to be an intellectual who, for recreation, read Homer and Plato and thus would be popular with the eggheads. Furthermore, he had always voted Republican and did not have any political charisma. Besides, no one asked McNamara if he was interested in the job which, for sure, he would not have accepted.

While Johnson was arranging his charades, a few of Bobby's friends attempted, in a rather haphazard manner, to start a boomlet. Unbeknownst to Bobby, Robert B. Shine, a New Hampshire Democrat and a public relations man, suddenly announced he was starting a write-in campaign. The President's blood pressure rose to an alarming degree once again, suspecting, as usual, that Bobby was the guiding force behind the move. Johnson immediately ordered Cliff Carter, one of his ace troubleshooters, to get in touch with Hugh Bownes, a power among the New Hampshire Democrats, and tell him to liquidate the boom. But Shaine could not be deterred. A few days later,

John King, the state's Democratic governor, joined with Shaine and asked all good Democrats to cast a vote for Bobby, suggesting at the same time that they also cast a ballot for Johnson. Bobby received 25,000 votes and Johnson about 29,000. In Johnson's mind, Bobby had received 25,000 votes too many.

Bobby was not happy with the New Hampshire operation, saying that it had been conducted in an amateurish way. Paul Corbin, for instance, had boasted that he would get Bobby on the national ticket, predicting that the next eight years would be Bobby's and the Bobby would be there in Washington all that time.

While Bobby deplored the activities of his well-meaning friends, he told his press agent, Ed Guthman, to release a statement five days before the primary to the effect that "the Attorney General has said that the choice of the Democratic nominee for Vice President will be made and should be made by the Democratic Convention in August, guided by the wishes of President Johnson and that President Johnson should be free to select his own running mate."

The two men spoke highly of each other in public. Bobby said that Johnson had "always been kind to me, to my family, and Mrs. Kennedy, both as Vice President and since then." In private, Johnson told a number of his Texan friends that he did not intend to tolerate Bobby's behavior nor that of the *Irish Mafia*. "If they try to push Bobby Kennedy down my throat for Vice President, I'll tell them to nominate him for the Presidency and leave me out of it." Of course, he had no intention of relinquishing the job nor the honors that went with it.

The time had long since passed for a light slap on Bobby's wrists— with *brickbats*. As a starter, Johnson told ex-Senator Scott Lucas of Illinois to start some action against Bobby in Massachusetts, to get all the delegates to put their John Doe to a pledge which read: "Be it resolved that President Lyndon B. Johnson, when nominated for President on the Democratic ticket, shall have the free choice of selecting his running mate as Vice President..."

It didn't work. When Douglas Carter tried to get the Democratic leaders in New Jersey and Rhode Island to get their colleagues to sign the pledge, they turned the suggestion down flat.

Resenting being dictated from the White House, they reminded Carter that the National Convention's duly-appointed delegates should have the privilege of voting for their choice in Atlantic City. Why have a convention at all, they asked, if the choice had already been made?

Johnson now tempted Senator Eugene McCarthy, the intellectual legislator from Minnesota. Ladybird Johnson thought Eugene was the right man for the job; the Johnson daughters, Lynda Bird and Luci, thought he was a "fantastic man." But McCarthy, too, was eliminated, leaving him somewhat bruised and resentful. It was now Humphrey's turn. The Minnesotan had been highly praised by Johnson, who in turn reacted in his usual enthusiastic manner. The build-up for Humphrey quickly began in earnest. On a speaking tour of the South, he did his best to convince businessmen that he was aware of their needs.

The time had now come to eliminate Bobby Kennedy. After discussing the strategy on how to accomplish that feat with Abe Fortas, Clark Clifford and James Rowe, Johnson decided to take the bull by the horns and beard the dangerous man from Massachusetts.

A week before the confrontation, Johnson held a press conference wherein he told the reporters that a Vice President "should be a man that is well received in all the states of the Union, among all our people. I would like to see a man that is experienced in foreign relations, and domestic affairs. I would like him to be a man of the people who felt a compassionate concern for their welfare and who enjoyed public service and was dedicated to it."

Although Bobby believed he fit the description, Johnson did not think he had compassion nor the expertise in domestic and foreign affairs. During the meeting, Johnson felt uneasy. Yet, he need not have been nervous, for Bobby, a gentleman in every respect, took the turndown gracefully. When Bobby asked Johnson whether he could be of service in the coming campaign, the President asked him to be his campaign manager. Bobby accepted and would resign as Attorney General, provided Johnson would nominate Nicholas Katzenback to take his place. The President, however, was not prepared for that. The deed done, the only thing remaining was to inform the public what had happened. Having no intentions of putting the bell on the cat, Johnson asked Kenneth O'Donnell, a close friend of Bobby's, to get him to publicly announce he was out of the race.

McGeorge Bundy, the cool, ex-Dean at Harvard University, on the other hand, willingly undertook the job. After hearing him out, Bobby told him to "go to hell," as he was not about to commit political *hari-kari* in public, forcing Johnson to handle the problem himself, through the following message:

"I have reached the conclusion that it would be inadvisable for me to recommend to the convention any member of my Cabinet or any of those who meet regularly with the Cabinet."

This primitive method to eliminate Bobby amazed everyone; it even shocked the public. The *Irish Mafia* expressed its feelings about Johnson in explosive terms: Johnson "shot us down, the son of a bitch."

The President was now in an exuberant state of mind. He rubbed a few pounds of salt in the *boy's* wounds, and had knocked him down with a few extra kicks for luck.

Two days after the confrontation, the President asked some of his favorite reporters to visit with him. He gave each a blow-by-blow description of the meeting with Bobby. To have heard him tell it, the *boy,* as he always called him, behaved like a frightened schoolboy caught by the truant officer on the way to the movies. He went so far as to describe the spasdomic movements of Bobby's Adam Apple.

Bobby learned about the press conference on his arrival at Hyannis Port. He was furious. Later, on seeing the President, Bobby accused him of having taped their meeting. Johnson denied it and swore that he had never whispered a word about their discussion to anyone. Labeling the President a "shameless fabricator," Bobby left and went home.

Chapter 24
A New Career

Bobby now began to think seriously about running for the United States Senate. The idea first blossomed when his brother-in-law, Stephen Smith, met John English, the Democratic Party leader in Nassau County, Long Island. The two met quite accidentally at a dedication of a school gymnasium being named after the late President. English, an aggressive and forward-looking politician, conveyed his thoughts to Smith, who wanted Bobby to run against Senator Kenneth Keating. Most of the old-line bosses who had not been able to elect a Democrat to a top legislative office in the state for over a decade saw magic in the Kennedy name. Some reform Democrats had doubts about Bobby's liberalism, and were reluctant at first to go along with their bosses. New York City Mayor Robert Wagner didn't like it either, afraid Bobby would take over the leadership of the party. Congressman Samuel Stratton called Bobby a carpetbagger, and The New York Times did not relish having Bobby run either. In an editorial, the paper stated:

"There is nothing illegal about the possible nomination of Robert F. Kennedy of Massachusetts as Senator from New York, but there is plenty that is cynical about it... The Attorney General has no special knowledge of New York's many complex problems; if he became a candidate, he would merely be choosing New York as a convenient launching pad for the political ambitions of himself and others."

Poor Senator Keating, the Republican incumbent, who had courageously stood up against Goldwater, and whose voting record had been liberal by most standards, now faced the end of his senatorial career. He may have displayed enough political courage to be mentioned in the book Profiles in Courage, but Bobby wasn't going to take time out to admire him, because by cutting Keating to pieces, he would become the third Kennedy to sit in the Senate.

Making haste to resign as Attorney General, he informed the press he was a candidate for the Senate.

Charles Buckley, the boss of the Bronx County Democrats, Stanley Steingut, the Democratic Party's overlord in Kings County, Peter Crotty, the upstate leader, and John English were in Bobby's corner. But the reformers were still unable to make up their collective minds. They could not understand how a man who always spoke about the new idealism in politics could team up with the old-line Democratic hacks. The problem was that they had not made a study of Boston politics. Practical young politicians on the make always use the hacks in *bean town* as long as they deliver. And, unlike Boston, the bosses in New York also commanded plenty of power.

There remained the problem of getting positive reaction from Mayor Wagner. Because Bobby had promised never to run for the Senate unless Wagner approved, the two men met at Gracie Mansion where, after several meetings, the Mayor decided to lend him his support. At City Hall, there were those who murmured at the strange turn of events. One politician described New York being over-run "just like Poland." Another activist who had helped Kennedy in former days said, "I don't like it at all. I would have been ready to fight but who did we have to fight with." Later on at the New York State Convention, a delegate moaned that she had to vote for Kennedy. "If I had any guts I'd vote for Stratton, but I don't want to get on the Kennedy hit list."

The 2,288 delegates and their alternates listened to the nomination speeches inside the 71st Regiment Armory. In stifling heat, as there was no air conditioning, Mayor Wagner kept on saying that he had entertained many doubts about Bobby, but that after hours of pondering, he concluded that Bobby was the best man the party could produce.

When the Band played the party's "unofficial anthem", instead of "Hello Lyndon" the crowd sang "Hello Bobby." John English stood on a chair and waved an extraordinary large wooden stick with three dozen balloons attached to it. When the demonstration subsided, New York Representative Otis G. Pike placed Samuel Stratton's name in nomination for the U.S. Senate. "Time after time," he wailed, "we have managed to snatch defeat from the jaws of victory. Our party in this state has been— is sick— until we make some changes.

"Two years ago, our leaders whipped out a well-known name, the illustrious son of an illustrious father, and we took one of the most illustrious shellackings of our illustrious history."

Stratton's supporters now poured into the aisles and staged a six minute demonstration, waving "Bobby Go Home" signs. But which home did they mean? Was it Washington D.C., Boston, Palm Beach, or the Bronx? Being that Stratton supporters couldn't tell, Bobby decided to stay. When the Stratton partisans retreated from the field, Under-Secretary of State W. Averill Harriman made a seconding speech on behalf of Bobby. Former New York City Police Commissioner Francis W. H. Adams, a Reform Democrat, spoke up for Stratton. And for some comic relief, Jose D. Alfaro, a 22 year old part-time college student from the 8th Assembly district in Queens, placed Adlai Stevenson's name in nomination.

At 4:30 p.m. the roll call began. Bobby's men were contacting delegates on the floor of the convention and winning them over much as what happened in the Los Angeles Presidential campaign.

Expected to get 200 votes, Stratton managed to hold on to the 29 delegates from Onandaga County, 10 from Schenectady and 16 from the New York delegation. Stratton had pleaded with the Democratic State Committee to take the necessary legal steps to keep Bobby off the ballot, but the Committee voted 232 to nine in favor of Bobby.

In his acceptance speech, Bobby promised to be worthy of the great sovereign State of New York. Then with Ethel by his side, he received the delegates and their wives at the Sheraton-Atlantic Hotel where the couple shook hands with all of their guests and then cut a six-tiered cake with "Welcome to New York" inscribed on it.

The campaign wasn't going to be an easy one. Because of his position on Goldwater, Senator Keating won the admiration of many Democrats and Republicans. A native son, he had the support of many liberals. Although Keating could call Bobby a carpetbagger, he soon discovered he had to contend with a super-powered political organization.

Invited to speak before the New York State AFL-CIO convention at the Commodore Hotel, Keating received only polite attention: he was a nice guy, up-standing citizen. On the following day, Kennedy spoke to the 1,500 union delegates, telling them that he was observing what was happening at the Republican Convention with considerable interest and amusement. "There was a man from Michigan making the nomination speech," he said referring to Thomas E. Dewey, "a man from Nebraska was chosen to direct the campaign (Herber Brownell), a former Congresswoman from Connecticut was ordered to get out of the race (Claire Booth Luce) by a former Senator from California (Richard Nixon) and the only thing they could agree on was that carpetbagger seemed a great issue in their favor." The delegates roared with laughter. "I need your help and assistance and I've come to ask for it."

"You're going to get it," a frog-voiced delegate shouted, and together with the others union leaders, they endorsed Bobby.

The Reform Democrats were still criticizing Bobby because of his doing business with the likes of Charles Buckley, the Bronx political boss. Bobby felt that something had to be done to win them over. At a meeting with the Reformers at the home of Lloyed Garrison, a prominent lawyer and leader of the group, they asked Bobby why he continued that relation. He answered that Buckly was his friend and that the Kennedy family was in his debt because he had supported John. They said the debt had been repaid in full when the President allowed Buckley to dole out federal jobs to the faithful party hacks. Refusing to turn on Buckley, Bobby promised to support Jonathan Bingham instead of Buckley for the congressional seat in the Bronx. At first they fumed and fretted, then finally came around to supporting Bobby.

The Kennedy organization opened its headquarters at 9 West 43rd Street in Manhattan with a large staff headed by Stephen Smith as manager. There were also David Hackett, Carmine Bellino, William F. Haddad and William J. Van der Heuvel. With the campaign chest amounting to only $1.5 million, Bobby knew the Democratic State Committee was in no position to make substantial contributions. This presented no serious problem. Bobby's family had planned to contribute handsomely. One advisor said, "We have a candidate who makes the money problem a lot less pressing."

Although money helped, Bobby received much more aid from people like Goldwater, who with his rash remarks had frightened thousands of moderate Republicans who were now voting Democrat. Although Keating was not a Goldwater admirer, nevertheless the people made their own connection. After all, politics and logic usually don't go well together.

The Republicans knew that Goldwater was a loser, but never imagined he could be drowned by a pro-Johnson avalanche of votes, many of which went to Bobby. And Keating wasn't helped any when the so-called Conservative Party put up Henry A. Paolucci, who drew 212,216 votes from the Republicans.

Neither Kennedy nor Keating discussed important issues. Keating was portrayed as a bumbling party hack, and Bobby as a carpetbagger and adventurer. Keating, moreover, pressed on one issue he thought was sure-fire: the General Aniline Case. He accused Bobby of authorizing the sale of Aniline to Interhandle, a Swiss corporation acting as a front for the German cartel, I.G. Farben. Washington lobbyists representing the Swiss corporation had been trying to pry General Aniline loose from the grasp of the alien Property Custodian. Drew Pearson wrote that "the staff of the Justice Department almost unanimously opposed the return of the property to the German owners which had so wantonly used slave labor and let them go to the gas chambers after they were no longer able to work". Despite Farben's past history, Bobby, without the approval of any Justice Department staff, ruled in favor of returning Aniline to the parent firm. Why did he decide to hand over the rich prize to Interhandle? According to Pearson, its Vice Chairman, William Payton Marin, who had approved the return to the original owners, was listed in *Who's Who* as a legal counsel for the Joseph P. Kennedy Enterprises. Pearson also revealed that Harold E. Clancy, an editor of the Boston Traveler, a newspaper that always favored Kennedy, was a director of the company, and discovered a memo in the files of the Justice Department, signed by Dr. Alfred Schaefer of Interhandle, which read: "We want to keep on dealing with Radziwill"— the Polish aristocrat who was a brother-in-law of Jacqueline Kennedy.

Serious issues aside, the staffs of both candidates were preoccupied in creating false images. Keating believed that he had an issue with the Farben case, but as we know, it turned out a dud. He challenged Bobby to debate the issues on television. And after purchasing time on a national network, Keating dared Bobby to appear in the studio with him. But Bobby was delivering speeches in Westchester County and was unable to appear. Keating had an empty chair placed in the studio to indicate that his opponent was afraid to debate. He also ordered the door be kept open just in case Bobby might arrive. Bobby, of course, was not to be seen.

A week later, the Republicans set up a similar telecast, and once more Keating dared Bobby to appear. This time Bobby showed up, posing for the television cameras outside the studio. While Keating held court inside, Bobby titillated the public with his version of the Farben affair— all at Keating's expense.

Bobby won the election by a majority of 719,693 votes, and Johnson captured the state with 2,669,517. After he had won, Bobby's friends informed him that the people no longer saw him as a ruthless man. Bobby smiled and said that this new image was just a figment in the minds of the Madison Avenue advertising hucksters.

"Now that I have won, I can go back to being ruthless again," he said slyly.

Chapter 25
Kennedy, New York's Senator

Members of the Senate maintain the patrician attitude of a Brutus or a Cicero of ancient Rome. And like the Romans, they brook no interference in the assertion of their prerogatives. Even a strong Chief Executive will think twice before bucking them as Woodrow Wilson dearly discovered in dealing with Senator Henry Cabot Lodge.

Although the power of the Presidency has grown enormously since Lodge battled the President, the Senate is still a world of its own, with Senators standing together like a brigade of legionaires, beating back any assault.

A new Senator is expected to be humble, and always ready to take lessons of decorum from his elders. Bobby, who had been the second most powerful man in the government, was expected to act accordingly.

Can Niagara Falls dry up?

Bobby, the meek politician?

With two Kennedys serving in the upper house, Bobby was sworn in on January 4, 1956, under the watchful eyes of Ethel, Teddy's wife Joan, Patricia Lawford, Jean Smith and four of Bobby's children. When a reporter asked Bobby what his feelings were, he said, "It will be a totally new life. I wouldn't be here unless I had wanted to come and I'm deeply committed. I was remembering and regretting the situation that gave rise to my being here."

He was fortunate in his committee assignments, having been chosen a member of the Labor and Public Welfare Committee of which Teddy was also a member along with Jacob Javits, the senior Senator from New York. Bobby was also assigned to the Committee on Government Operations and to the District of Columbia Committee where he would able to do something for underprivileged black youths in the capital. None of the assignments were of a prestigious caliber, but much more than a junior Senator was usually granted by the men controlling the

Senate.

Many of his colleagues called Bobby just *No. 99*,i.e., next to the last man— his good friend Senator Joseph D. Tyding Jr. of Maryland. One of the older Senators commented that it was "just too bad for Bobby, We operate under the seniority system not by a system of blood relatives." Another Republican pointed out that Bobby always had photographers around when he visited his brother's grave, emphasizing the fact that he went there twice during the course of each day. Cynics even carped about Bobby's climbing a mountain named for his brother: "Mountain climbing is fine when Congress is not in session, but New York's legislation is important and he should have been here," one of them said. Others objected to Bobby's abrasive ways because they knew he would never play the game according to the rules. After all, Bobby was a national figure, one who reminded people of the late President both in gesture and in action.

Teddy, on the other hand, was popular with the Senators. An extrovert, he could backslap with the best of them and enjoy having a glass of bourbon with an Eastland, whereas Bobby's shattering candor did not endear him to too many legislators. Teddy was simply "nice." One Democratic colleague made this distinction: "Teddy talks to you and wants to know what he can do for you. Bobby looks like he's ready to cut someone's gizzard out."

If Bobby had his way, he would have no qualms in cutting out Javits' gizzard. Not only did Bobby not defer to the senior Senator, he made it a point to make Javits look like an ineffective bumbler who should be retired to an old age home.

Shriver, the Director of the Office of Economic Opportunity, gave both Senators a 45-minute notice that $390,000 would be appropriated to clean up a Harlem slum area. While Bobby's Adam Walinsky wrote a release in about 20 minutes, Javits' staff was slow on the ball. At the joint press conference, therefore, Bobby managed to get all the headlines. To this day, Javits believes that Shriver had told Bobby all about it beforehand.

On another occasion, when he learned that the federal government had made a substantial grant to the City of Syracuse, Bobby immediately went to Syracuse, to make the announcement, once again beating Javits to the punch. Now, Javits was certain that Shriver was tipping Bobby off.

Bobby also criticized New York Governor Nelson Rockefeller's handling of the program to rehabilitate narcotic addicts, saying that the governor hadn't "gotten off [his] tail yet." Javits, of course, had been one of the originators of that program. When asked if he was ridiculing his Republican colleagues, Bobby said he had no intention of slighting anyone. His rejoinder, however, did not impress many. It was a well known fact that neither he nor Javits trusted each other, and that both had spies trying to find out what plots were being hatched to embarass the other.

With a staff of 30, he had them research every conceivable subject under the sun, preparing dozens of releases and writing speeches for every occasion.

He had a great deal to say about the "deplorable state of public education," striking against those who operated on the premise "that there was no need for a change." He suggested that student records, particularly of those receiving federal aid, be looked at on a regular basis to determine whether they were improving in their studies. Praised by many eminent educators, Bobby had an amendment passed which granted a large sum of money to primary and secondary educational institutions. He also introduced an amendment to the Johnson Aid-To-Appalachia Bill (also called the Anti-Poverty Bill) which called for the allocation of $840 million for road building and several hundred million dollars for water conservation, sewage projects and vocational training for the underprivileged in an 11 states area designated as the Appalachia region.

Rockefeller didn't want his state included in that bill because it would reflect on his stewardship. Instead, he plugged for funds to build a super-highway that would traverse the southern-tier counties along Western Pennsylvania. Through this project, Rockefeller would bring new business into the region and lift the standard of living for the inhabitants. Bobby proposed that the 13 counties should be included.

In a convincing speech, he said that he had become disturbed about poverty ever since he had conducted the primary campaign for his brother in West Virginia. Knowing that Bobby was shooting at Rockefeller, Javits listened with increasing impatience. In his mind he felt that Bobby was saying that a New York Senator and its governor had been remiss in attending to the needs of the lower-income groups. After receiving 10 minutes of time from Bobby, Javits explained that the wording of his amendment would lead many to think that he wanted the poverty region to include territory right up to the Canadian border, that Bobby had neglected to include the names of the counties. He further reminded Bobby that the initial bill required the governors of these states to be consulted beforehand. He then asked Bobby to agree to an amendment on top of his own, which would call for a "consultation with the governor." Bobby not only concurred; he went a step further. He promised to expurgate all the unflattering remarks he had made about Rockefeller from the Congressional Record. As a result, Bobby was featured in the newspapers and over television as a man dedicated to the interests of the people.

He enjoyed the rivalry, especially getting the jump on Javits. It happened again over a bill which Bobby pushed through— the right to vote, which would affect about 500,000 Puerto Ricans. Unable to vote because they did not know enough English, Bobby asked that any man or woman with a sixth grade education be allowed to vote— thus eliminating the requirement of English language skills. But although the amendment passed the Senate, it was voted down by the House. Later however, the leaders of both bodies met and ironed out their differences. With Bobby's essentials remaining in the bill, he now got the Puerto Rican population firmly in his fold.

As a Senator, Bobby cut his wisdom teeth, and his staff under Joseph Dolan was considered one of the best on the Hill. His two bespectacled assistants, Adam Walinsky and Peter Edelman, wrote his speeches and advised him on foreign policy. There were also Wes Barthelmes, a reporter for the *Washington Post,* and Angela M. Novello, the trusted secretary.

His four room, modestly furnished suite contained an oil portrait of his brother Lt. Joseph Jr.; a picture of a Navy destroyer named after Joe Jr.; a photograph of his parents and children with their respective spouses and offsprings; a photograph of Bobby atop a ski slope, and one of his children deep in prayer. There was also a picture of rotund President William Howard Taft standing alongside Mayor *Honey Fitz,* his grandfather; another of the members of the Hoover Commission; one of his father bearing an inscription of the former President, plus a picture of Harry S. Truman with Ted; still another of Bobby chatting with John Glenn, the Astronaut; finally, one of the poet Robert Frost. There were of course many photographs of John F. Kennedy, and an impressive looking painting of John standing before a joint session of the Congress. There was framed in a black border a sheet of ruled yellow legal paper of John's doodling and notations he had made during a cabinet meeting on October 29, 1963, which read: "For Robert Kennedy from Jackie. Lastly, there was a photograph of Bobby's oldest son, Joseph, sitting near the White House fountain with the following inscription: "A future President inspects his property," signed "John F. Kennedy."

When asked how it felt to be a Senator, Bobby answered: I enjoyed the first months more than I thought I would. The matters I became involved in were those which I was deeply interested in and which really meant something to me— housing, education and the poverty programs. It was all worthwhile. And all the Senators were most considerate."

Chapter 26
The Morrisey Case

A short time after Bobby had informed Zaretski that the Kennedys were not in the habit of giving political hacks important jobs, both Bobby and Ted sponsored Francis K. Morrisey, an old family retainer, for a federal judgeship. Morrisey had other friends including Cardinal Cushing, John McCormack and members of the Massachusetts Bar Association.

Bobby asked President Johnson to appoint him to the bench, saying that his late brother had intended to present Morrisey with the job after Congress had passed the necessary legislation to create 70 additional vacancies for the federal courts. Bobby, however, did not tell the President that the Massachusetts and the National Bar Associations did not favor the appointment. Johnson agreed and presented his name for consideration to the Senate Judiciary Committee.

Tom Wicker, *New York Times* columnist, wrote that Morrisey was "lacking in any qualifications to be a federal judge save long political service to the Kennedys [and] by allowing the appointment to be pushed as far as they did, Johnson suffered a grievous loss of prestige and dignity and that all of them opened themselves to the charge of damaging the whole federal bench by being willing to elevate an unqualified and inappropriate man to it."

The news of the impending appointment aroused the ire of Chief Justice Charles Wyzanski of Massachusetts, who declared that he could not "overlook the obvious fact that the only discernible ground for the nomination of Morrisey was his service to the Kennedy family."

With Ted the "front man" in the operation, Bobby was busy lining up Democratic votes for the would-be judge. When several people asked why he was supporting the appointment of one so obviously unqualified, Bobby became indignant, saying that "as these stories have made him appear I would never have recommended his nomination and President Johnson would never have made it. I would suggest that before Morrisey is accused, tried and convicted in absentia, he have the opportunity to appear before the Senate and answer to his qualifications." Soon, Morrisey got his chance.

Testifying on his own behalf, Morrisey admitted that he had failed to pass the bar examination twice, that he had planned to practice law in Georgia, but that after struggling for several months, he went back to Boston where he enrolled as a student at Suffolk Law School an earned an M.A. degree, and that he passed his bar examination the third time around. He also stated that he ran in the primaries as a candidate for the Massachusetts House of Representatives, finishing sixth in a field of nine.

In a series of articles in *The Boston Globe*, the authors noted a number of contradictions in the Morrisey testimony. According to the writer, Morrisey had no legal right to stand as a candidate because of his purported residence in Georgia, during that period: "The disclosure becomes pertinent because by his own testimony before the U.S. Senate Judiciary Committee has made his whereabouts in 1933-34 a central issue in his fight for confirmation."

According to his statements, Morrisey placed himself in Georgia from June 1933 to March 1934, and the Massachusetts State Constitution required that a candidate must have one year residence in a district before he could legally represent it.

When a Senator asked him if he had considered himself to be a legal resident of Georgia, he answered, "I did when I was down there."

Albert E. Jenner, the chairman of the Judiciary Selection Committee of the American Bar Association, gave a different version: "Morrisey, while a resident of Boston, had within a two-day period traveled to Georgia, received his diploma from a Southern law school and had been admitted without examination to the state and federal courts in Georgia."

Morrisey's conflicting statements and the information about his strange career supplied by the Bar Associations led Senator Everett Dirsksen to call for a closed hearing: "We've got to look at it, you just can't blink at such things."

By that time, the Senators questioned Morrisey's veracity. The would-be judge admitted that his omission of many facts on how he had acquired his law degree "had been an unwise omission." Dirksen went after him with a fervor which made Morrisey tremble with fear. He hinted at "some pretty damaging evidence" which he would reveal if Morrisey persisted in trying to get himself appointed to the bench. But Morrisey showed no signs of retiring gracefully. Dirksen exhibited copies of articles published in *Il Mattino* of Naples, and in *Il Tempo* of Rome about a serious incident on the Isle of Capri.

While the Morrisey family and that of Ted Kennedy were vacationing, Morrisey met with Albert Spinella, a *mafioso* and an alleged criminal who had been deported from the U.S. because he had been accused of murder, armed robbery and sundry other crimes. The newspapers reported that Spinella had lunch with Kennedy and Morrisey at the exclusive Hotel Quisisano: "It seemed that the [undesirable] found favor in the eyes of the Kennedys who engaged him as a *cicerone* (tour guide) and then as dining companion at the noted restaurant."

Dirksen said he had all 32 Republican Senators lined up to vote against Morrisey's confirmation, and a Democratic spokesman said that 13 of their men planned to take diplomatic absences. Morrisey surely would have lost.

With the final count taken, Ted phoned President Johnson to inform him that he had decided to recommit the nomination on his own volition but failed to let his Democratic colleagues know about his sudden change of mind. He did step across the aisle to speak with Dirksen. Hubert Humphrey, and his good friends who had labored to have Morrisey confirmed, were very embarrassed at the sudden turn of events.

After apologizing to Dirksen, Ted delivered a heart-rending speech which brought forth copious tears from the many tender-hearted legislators. It would have gone better with a Mississippi river boat audience: Morrisey had been poor— one of 12 children. His father was a dock worker, the family living in a home without gas, electricity or heat in the bedroom— their shoes held together by wooden pegs their father had made. " As a child of this family, Judge Morrisey could not afford to study law full time," Kennedy said.

The Kennedy brothers put the prestige of the federal courts on the line. When President Johnson sponsored an unqualified man to serve on the bench, he did a great deal to tarnish its reputation. Observers thought that Johnson had played a clever game by agreeing to appoint Morrisey, certain he would have discredited Bobby. But as things turned out, it did nothing to enhance either the President's reputation or that of the Kennedy brothers.

Chapter 27

The Manchester Affair

The days had long passed since Bobby could pick up the phone and tell his brother at the White House what to do when crises arose. Johnson surely was not one to pay heed to Bobby's suggestions, in any event.

Bobby was greatly disturbed by the landing of the U.S. Marines in the Dominican Republic, to save the country from communism by propping up an anti-Bosch Military Junta.

In a speech on the floor, he said, "I am sure that every member of this body agrees with President Johnson in his determination to prevent the establishment of a new Communist state in this hemisphere. The free republics of the Americas have solemnly declared communism to be incompatible with the inter-American system. Action against revolutions aiming to install Communist regimes is in the interests of the whole hemisphere. But this cannot mean that we plan to act on our own without regard to our friends and allies in the Organization of American States. In recent years we have established a relationship of mutual trust and confidence between the United States and the free republics of the hemisphere. There is nothing more important to our future in the hemisphere than the preservation and strengthening of these bonds of mutual affection and respect.

"Since we believe in the rule of the law, we must always take care to respect the sovereignty of other nations; to proceed on the basis of our obligation to each other and to make sure that we continue to strengthen the structure of law in the hemisphere."

He criticised the unilateral action taken by the Johnson Administration and suggested that the country would be in a much stronger position if it would "act in concert with the rest of the hemisphere... Consultation is the price we must pay for the extra strength our alliance gives us." He then stressed that the "determination to stop communism in the hemisphere must not be construed as opposition to popular uprisings against injustice and oppression just because the targets of such popular uprisings say they are Communist-inspired or Communist-led, or even because known Communists take part in them... Our objective must surely be not to drive the genuine democrats in the Dominican revolution into association with the Communists by blanket characterization and condemnation of their revolution, but rather to isolate the Communists by assuring the genuine Democrats, including those who took part in the revolution, will have a future in the rebuilding of their country."

He now made plans to tour Latin America to ascertain the facts. Before leaving, he talked to Jack Hood Vaughn, the Assistant Secretary of State. Vaughn asked Bobby not to criticize government policy in the Dominican Republic. But Bobby was determined to meet the issue head on.

Speaking in Lima, Peru, he said that "if a country votes to have a Communist government, and no country has voted for one since World War II, then there will be no intervention like there was in the Dominican Republic... I disagree with the intervention, but it must be seen in perspective. The United States does not want to dominate the Dominican Republic. It wants no military bases there. If the people want a Communist government we will stay out."

Wherever he went, he repeated the same statement, but no one really believed that the United States would not intervene if a government with leftist leanings was about to take over power in any country south of the border.

In Cuzco, Peru, he was overwhelmed by an army of begging children. The thin-legged, pot-bellied, malnourished urchins ripped Bobby's trousers and injured his face as they pushed him against a barbed wire fence.

Having told the press that the trip was "an unofficial, privately-financed, fact-finding mission," and that he had decided to go to Latin America to reassure the people, because "the Alliance of Progress was still alive and important as it was under President John F. Kennedy."

In Lima, he found the Alliance "had been slower than we hoped, less certain than we expected, but is is in progress." In Santiago, Chile, reporters asked him if he was going after the Presidential nomination in 1968. He said that he supported Johnson for re-election. When they wanted to know if he would be a candidate for the office in 1972, he answered "that's a long way off." He told the reporters that he would announce it should the candidacy develop," but he took pains to assure them that Johnson was doing "an outstanding job."

On November 26, Dean Rusk was spat upon by a 25-year

old student in Montevideo, just as he was about to lay a wreath at the foot of the monument of General Jose Antigas, a revered national hero. While Rusk wiped the saliva off his face, the student shouted: "This in the name of my people."

About the same time, Bobby was having a rough experience in Chile. A number of students called him "an assassin." Not stopping at name-calling, they hurled eggs, rocks and money, screaming, "Yankee Go Home." After 20 minutes of continued shouting, Bobby finally was able to be heard. He asked some students to step up to the platform to discuss the issues in a "rational fashion." They, instead, asked him to go to them. As he approached, they kicked him in the shins while others burned the American flag. Finally, when they calmed down to a degree, they told him that their grievance was solely directed at the United States Government whose politics "we are unable to accept."

At a local steel mill, whose workers were mostly Socialists or Communists, he was challenged to climb down a rickety ladder to examine a blast furnace at close range. "Of all people here, I have to meet this one," he exclaimed. He climbed down the ladder, looked at the furnace, and then made a speech in which he said that Chile must "decide for itself what sort of government was best for the country." Then, he urged the men to support the program of President Eduardo Frei Montava, the Christian Democratic leader. In Linares, he was again asked about his plans to run the Presidency. A mob of admirers almost crushed him to death. While trying to extricate himself from its enthusiastic embraces, he sang *The Battle Hymn of the Republic.* Impressed by the number of schools established under the Alliance for Progress, he made sure that the people knew that one out of every five children in Chile was fed through the Food for Peace operation. Under questioning, he admitted that the Alliance had not progressed fast enough under his brother, but that Johnson "had been placing too much emphasis on stopping communism" and not enough on what he called "non-violent revolutions now taking place in South America."

He dissassociated himself from the Administration's action in the Dominican Republic— a very definite gain. On Vietnam, he was asked why he had not spoken out more boldly against the war and against the policy of the government.

"I happen to have some disagreement with President Johnson on Vietnam," he said, and stopped without further elaboration.

Back home, in *Harper's Magazine,* on October 1966, William V. Shannon said that Bobby was seeking the Vice Presidency: "With skilful publicity this could be made to appear not as an act of bold usurpation and impatient ambition by Kennedy but a reluctant rescue mission to prop up an aging President whose popularity is sagging."

Shannon believed that it could succeed. The tactic to swing to the left of the opposition was the very same one that Johnson used when he ran against Goldwater. Not only was he moving to the left, he was outflanking Humphrey, who had entrapped himself into playing the role of a Charlie McCarthy to Johnson's Bergen.

The Wall Street Journal made a study of Bobby's political activities (October 17, 1966) and found that Bobby "has been careful of late to avoid sharp attacks on the President. When he expressed doubts about the Vietnam policy, he always stresses that "these are very complex problems with no simple solutions."

The very sensitive President was concerned about the Bobby phenomena, afraid that *the boy* (other times he called him the *little shit*) was about to take over the Democratic Party and check in as a permanent resident at the White House in 1968.

Their associates didn't help matters either. They spread all kinds of stories about Johnson and Bobby. One had Johnson walk into the office of Senator Dirksen where a number of Republican legislators were making small talk until Johnson opened up on John Kennedy, saying that the so-called leader would have fallen flat on his face if he, Johnson, wasn't around to hold him up. The Republicans were embarrassed at the outburst, but the story spread far and wide.

Another story had Bobby's friends making fun of Johnson's oratorical style and "limited outlook," calling him *Colonel Cornpone.*

Despite the antipathy, Bobby and the President kept up appearances in public. But when *Look Magazine* began to serialize a *Portrait Of A President: John F. Kennedy In Profile* by William Manchester, things changed dramatically. Among other things, Manchester made Johnson appear like a crude, vulgar lout, one who managed to step on everyone's toes while en-route from Dallas to Washington after John F. Kennedy's assassination. On the plane he supposedly ensconced himself in Jackie's private compartment, sprawled over her bed dictating to Marie Hahner, his secretary. When Jackie appeared in the doorway, he got up and shuffled out.

On January 10, 1967, Governor Connally, a close friend of

141

the late President, said that John F. Kennedy had gone to Texas to regain some of his sagging popularity. In commenting about the Manchester book, he said it was an, "astonishing propaganda instrument woven to reflect favorably on those who gave it birth while rudely discreditory to others involved... It is filled with editorial comment based on unfounded rumors, distortion, inconsistency. This transparent attempt to dictate history through a captive voice is shocking. It is a recitation of recollections and observations collected and reflected through the prism of prejudice."

Another Johnson spokesman was convinced that the main purpose of the book was to "destroy Johnson. They are going to try and make him out to be some kind of monster."

On December 17, 1966, William H. White, Johnson's journalist friend, said, "The President has had to bear a frightful burden in the unrelenting hostility of the Kennedy cult and the attitude that the man in the White House is not simply a constitutional successor to another man slain in a memorable tragedy but only a crude usurper. Any mature newsman in Washington knows that this is the plain truth. Every writer in the United States and every publisher knows it too, that the smile or the frown of the cult has a power over the fortunes of any kind of book that this country has never known before."

Then, an alleged highly-placed authority was quoted as saying, "It is my firm belief that if the Kennedys allow the manuscript to be published in 1967, it will be a clear signal that Bobby intends to challenge Lyndon B. Johnson for the Democratic Presidential nomination in 1968."

Another associate was quoted as saying that "Bobby was trying to use Bobby Baker, Billie Sol Estes and the Johnson radio and TV stations in Austin in an effort to convince John F. Kennedy to dump Johnson and O'Donnell was hoping to turn the trip into an anti-Johnson show to prove that he has lost control in his own state."

Johnson's supporters weren't through. Texans believe in doing things in a big way. After berating Bobby, Jackie and O'Donnell about the plane trip and criticism in the Manchester book, they began to leak stories about the funeral arrangements. One of Johnson's men said that "the entire series of events had been a calculated, contrived, emotional buildup not for the sake of paying honest respect to and showing genuine grief for John F. Kennedy, but to enhance the Kennedy family and the Kennedy name."

After stressing Johnson's concern about the Kennedy public image, that spokesman hastened to assure all those within the range of his voice that "Johnson didn't desert the Kennedy program. He carried it on and did a lot better with it in Congress, in the business community and everywhere else than Jack could have, and now the President is getting the feeling that the Kennedy program got him into trouble in the last election by trying to go too far too fast."

That was damning the late President with faint praise. The spokesman was saying that Kennedy was an "inept" executive who had saddled a program on an "able" Chief Executive. The Freudian slip revealed more than was intended.

The Johnson people were trying to make the Kennedys appear like Madison Avenue hucksters who had only one thing on their minds: to use the funeral to further Bobby's ambitions. They also managed to reveal their essential provincialism when they described the funeral as a European style affair. What they were saying was that Bobby was a cold, calculating politician who didn't care one inch about his older brother, but was only concerned about getting into the White House. It was manifestly unfair of them to accuse him of being a heartless, ambitious operator, who was putting on a good emotional show just to impress the public with the depth of his grief. And it was unfair of the Texans to say that Jackie, Bobby and their friends were busily concocting schemes to use the funeral for so sordid a purpose. To most Americans, the bereaved family acted in a perfectly normal way. To many, they were solemnly courageous. And it was expected that they, and they alone, should be in charge of the funeral arrangements.

Bobby and Jackie have been harshly criticised about their attitude towards Texans in general. But they had their reasons. On May 29, 1965, for example, the 48th anniversary of John F. Kennedy's birth, the Texas House of Representatives defeated by a record vote of 72 to 52, with Governor Connally's brother voting with the majority, a bill which had been passed unanimously in the state Senate proposing to rename the state school for the mentally retarded at Richmond in President Kennedy's honor.

Although the Manchester book showed a visible bias against Johnson and his entourage, it also reported problems with the Kennedys themselves. Schlesinger got into the controversy head on. On one hand he defended the Kennedys; on the other he criticized Manchester, presenting the case against the author like a Philadelphia lawyer and not like a highly-regarded historian, causing many critics to come to the front. One said that Manchester was no stray or wicked eavesdropper. He had been chosen by Bobby, Jackie and the family to

143

write a "scrupulous history and he has known for his ardent devotion to John F. Kennedy. If he could not record events as the Kennedys would like to be remembered what would satisfy them!"

Bobby was caught in a trap as he was being hurt politically by all the washing of dirty linen in public. He could have avoided some embarrassment if he had said that he was not in sympathy with the book's political judgment and had refrained from imposing his views on the author. If the suspicious Chief Executive would still express his doubts about Bobby's aims in having the book written in the first place, the public would have accepted his version of the affair and viewed him as a victim of circumstances.

Why did Bobby choose that author in the first place? "What happened," he explained, "was that in 1964 we started hearing that three or four sensational writers were starting to work on books. I mean the sort of writer that would sensationalize the story, who would dwell on that sort of detail that served no real purpose.

"We just didn't want to go through it all over and over again. I suppose we were naive, because we're going to have to live with this thing the rest of our lives. But in January of '64 we thought we could have one man do it, and have it done with.

"Most of this reasoning came from Pierre and it was Pierre who suggested Manchester. I had never met Manchester before."

Theodore White, author of *The Making of a President*, and Walter Lord, who had written *A Night To Remember* and *Day of Infamy*, were approached to write the Kennedy book. White turned it down because he felt too deeply about the tragedy. Later, he said that "those of us who write of public affairs would do almost anything rather than sign such a contract." Lord, who had been contacted by Edwin O. Guthman, was Bobby's press secretary at the Justice Department; he, too, said no.

Manchester, therefore, was asked to write the book. He was associated with the American Educational Publications at Wesleyan University, and was also engaged in writing a book about the Krupp munitions empire.

A few years later, when the relations between Bobby and Manchester reached the breaking point, the latter remarked bitterly, "I didn't come to you, you came to me. I was perfectly happy writing the book I was interested in doing. Arthur Schlesinger talked to me about the book; Salinger talked to me about the book. This book has ruined my life, my family life is not the

144

same. I've been under a doctor's care."

The memo binding the agreement between Manchester and the Kennedys was signed by Bobby on March 26, 1964. It stipulated, among other things, that "the completed manuscript shall be reviewed by Mrs. John Kennedy and Robert F. Kennedy and the final text should not be published unless and until approved by them." It also stated that "other rights may be disposed of by Manchester with the approval of the Kennedys though it is not the intention to prevent the sale of serial option rights to a responsible publisher." Other items in the contract called for a publishing date to be not earlier than November 22, 1968, after the national elections, unless Mrs. Jacqueline Kennedy gave him permission to have the book published earlier. He had to promise to treat the material he had received from his exclusive right to interview the Kennedys with the "utmost discretion," and that if Jacqueline or Robert Kennedy were unable to give final approval to the manuscript "such approval shall be given to Senator Edward P. Kennedy or someone he designates."

The agreement read plain enough. But Manchester gave his own interpretation.

When the ruckus reached its highest intensity, Pierre Salinger entered the fray and contributed his mite to the Donnybrook. He declared that Manchester "is purely and simply a welcher who welched on his contract. He sought $665,000 and ratted on his contract. This has nothing to do with changing history, no matter what some misguided author up in Connecticut may think or say. And you mày quote me on that!"

During that period Bobby had remarked that the book would not be published for at least 25 or 50 years. He certainly had no intention of having it published in 1969 or 1970. "It would look like something turned out just to help me, with all the talk of running for the Presidency in 1972."

One fact could not be refuted: he *did* assist Manchester in selling the serial rights; he also had told a friend that the Kennedy-Manchester differences would never be brought into court because it would make the "family look like book burners." Since the story got out that the Kennedys would not like to bring any court action against Manchester, his position was weakened to some extent. Bobby said that "they thought it would be too politically dangerous for me, if the whole thing was brought into court."

The entire project not only was ill-conceived from the very beginning, it also had too many inputs from too many people. Early in April 1966, Edwin O. Guthman and John Siegenthaler, experienced journalists and longtime associates of Bobby, scrutinized the raw manuscript, as did Arthur Schlesinger Jr. and Richard Goodwin. The latter suggested that the title be changed from *Death of a Lancer* (Lancer was the Secret Service code name for John F. Kennedy) to *The Death of a President.* He also said that five pages should be cut towards the end of the book and that a direct quote by Jackie should also be eliminated. Furthermore, he thought that the book as a whole was good but some prose was sloppy and maudlin, and that Johnson had been viciously portrayed.

On May 16, Evan Thomas, the Harper and Row top executive, wrote to Siegenthaler and Guthman: "The book was in part tasteless and gratuitously insulting to President Johnson and even to the memory of the late President Kennedy. That marvelous Irish politician, who became one of the world's great statesmen, is almost deprived of his miraculous self, is seen as the child of Arthur and Guinevere while Black Jack Bouvier's daughter is somehow deprived of her hard-won stature by being born of elves in a fairy glade by being dressed in magic cloth of gold.

"The Texans in their polka-dot dresses and bow ties are seen as newly-arrived scum plucked from the dung heep by magical Jack."

After venting his spleen on the author because of his treatment of the Texans, Thomas admitted that "this is a good book. I can't see any publisher leaving any stone unturned no matter what the consequences, and there will be bloody consequences when the truly-dedicated Manchester comes across the markings..."

Schlesinger now contributed some carping of his own. He did not like to see the late President as "a man who resents shooting deer and is preoccupied with the decor of his office and his wife's clothes... [That was] not the Kennedy I knew." Schlesinger had of course forgotten that he had written a very graphic description of the President weeping in his wife's room when the invading Cubans had been defeated by Castro's men.

The storm broke out in a renewed fury when Don Congdon, Manchester's literary agent, started peddling the serial rights to magazines.

With *Look magazine* having been chosen, Warren Rogers, the publication's Washington editor, was instructed to get in touch with Bobby to ask him if he had any objections about the book being serialized.

"*Look* had been good to us and vice versa," Bobby said. Then he told Rogers to talk to Siegenthaler and Guthman: "Call

John, and if there is anything else I can do let me know."

In the meantime, while all that was going on, Manchester was brooding in Middletown, Connecticut. He was now certain that the book would never be published. Disturbed by his evident state of mind, Evan Thomas asked Bobby's friend to get "Bob to write a letter to Manchester saying that the book would be published in 1968 or whatever... He's getting despondent over all the changes."

Bobby did send Manchester a letter assuring him that the book would be published. When some of his friends asked him why he had put himself on record, he said, "They told me the man was sick, that he might jump out of a building or something."

It was at that time that Bobby and Jackie learned that Manchester had signed a contract with *Look Magazine*. One of Kennedy's friends asked Manchester why he had not cleared it with the family. The writer assured him that he had not signed any contract. For reasons unknown, Bobby's letter never reached Manchester, who was becoming upset to the point of a breakdown.

On July 28, Bobby sent a letter to the author, telling him that he hadn't read the book but had the utmost faith in his "abilities as an historian and reporter," mentioning that other writers were about to give their versions on what had happened in Dallas and that it was imperative that the book should be published because it was based on material which the family made available to him, further assuring the author that no difficulties would be put "in the way of publication of the work."

Then the lawyers came in. Simon H. Rifkind, represented the Kennedys and John F. Harding *Look Magazine*. William Attwood and Gardner Cowles also got into the act to try to find a rational way out of the dilemma. Rifkind objected to the serialization and about the publication date which had been set for sometime in November. Coles received a call from Jackie, who felt that November was "always a difficult time for me and the children and could [he] postpone serialization." Cowles was agreeable and promised to talk to Evans Thomas.

Rifkind again mentioned that the serialization was disturbing the family and that it should be discontinued. Bobby was more blunt: "Tear up the contract and forget the whole business." Cowles turned that suggestion down cold. "I bought a property with your full approval, and I don't see why I should tear up a contract because you've had a change of heart."

The arguments between them were becoming more acrimonious. Jackie kept on repeating, "I can't understand. I can't understand why you should go ahead contrary to my wishes."

After a long and exhausting session, a compromise was reached— or so they all thought! Cowles phoned Goodwin and asked him if Manchester had been contacted to get his approval of the cuts. Goodwin told him that no one had discussed the matter with the author. On September 7, Manchester arrived at Hyannis Port to talk about changes with Goodwin and the Kennedys. Goodwin wanted Manchester to cut out all references placing Johnson in a bad light. The author refused, saying that he was willing to eliminate all copy pertaining to any personal information which Jackie found objectionable. He phoned Don Congdon to send the magazine and book galleys up by plane. Manchester left Hyannis Port. An hour later, Goodwin drove to the airport to pick up the galleys, surprised to learn that the author had ordered the copies sent back to New York. Jackie, Bobby and Goodwin were furious. They thought that Manchester was not acting in good faith.

The last meeting between the contending parties, before Manchester sailed for England, took place at Bobby's pool at his McLean, Virginia home. Manchester found it disconcerting talking with Bobby, who insisted on talking while swimming. Nevertheless, Bobby told Manchester that "it would be intolerable to have Jackie as a witness in the trial. For another, I'd be in the business of suppressing a book. I can't stand that kind of a fight."

Everyone was having a hand in changing the manuscript. Goodwin cut out a number of lines. Mike Land of *Look* flew over to London and got Manchester to delete more material. Evan Thomas came to London armed with a letter from Jackie, asking the author to cut 27 more items. But all the traveling and effort proved fruitless. Not satisfied, Jackie insisted on starting a law suit, unbeknownst to Bobby, who, on hearing about it, turned pale, but had to along with her decision. Fortunately, an agreement was finally reached. Manchester permitted the publisher to cut 1,600 words out of the original manuscript. But the brawl was far from over.

It took on international flavor when the rights to serialize the book had been sold to a number of European magazines. When Henri Nannen, the editor of *Der Stern*, was asked to go along with the new agreement, he balked, insisting that he was within his rights to print the material as it had been written. There would be no expurgated edition of the book if he could help it. And the German law protected him from the assaults of the Kennedys.

Nannen was now in a talkative mood, and intended to speak out about whatever was in his mind. He said it was remarkable to read the various stories about the sensational material in the book which were being printed in the newspapers: "Remarkable because the clumsiness with which Senator Kennedy handled this case corresponds not at all to the political style of this outstanding family. Did he really think he could manipulate all the quarrels between the Kennedy clan and the Johnson supporters out of Manchester's writing— only so that Johnson would keep the President's chair warm for another four years!"

He mentioned that when William Attwood refused to go along, Bobby stopped sending him Christmas cards.

Nannen criticised the choice of deletions. Instead of a wrinkle which Jackie had discovered on her face, the wording was changed to "she found she looked tired." In the Manchester copy itemizing the contents of her purse, he mentioned that "cigarettes" were included. That word was eliminated. In describing that she spent an hour making up, the new version read "a long time."

Nannen thought that Jackie had been put in a difficult position. She would not act as a normal young woman but only in a way that would help Bobby further his ambitions to become President.

It was the editor's contention that Bobby and Jackie ordered that 7,000 words deleted from the manuscript for political reasons. His greatest fear, he said, was that nothing that served to indicate his hostile feelings towards Johnson should be printed before the 1968 election. The book could lead to a defeat for Johnson and the election of a Republican, and that could cause a deferment of Bobby's plan to become President by 1972, at the latest.

That was his original idea, as Nannen saw it. But Bobby's election as a U.S. Senator made him alter his blueprint. It was quite clear that the Kennedy name was a potent factor. The Vietnam War was eroding Johnson's popularity, and the civil rights question has weakened the President, with small property owners who feared a Negro invasion into their neighborhoods because of the fair-housing act. Bobby, Nannen said, now changed his target date to 1968. The German surmised that Bobby had given Manchester a go-ahead signal to have the book published earlier because he thought the time to strike out against Johnson was now, not later.

An article in *U.S. News and World Report* November 1968, made Bobby change his plans again, according to the editor. He discovered that the real purpose of the Anti-Johnsonites was to split the party wide open. Teddy Roosevelt had done the same to the Republican Party after he thought he had been betrayed by Taft and the opposition party won the election as a result. Bobby decided not to have history repeat itself, and went back to his original plan. Nannen said that Bobby had no intention of instituting a suit against the book publisher or *Look:* "Jackie simply ran out of control."

Nannen said that he had never been told about the deletions and did not learn what had been penciled out until he received the manuscript on January 3. When Bobby discovered that the German editor did not intend to go along with him, he began a high pressure campaign to bring Nannen into line.

Bobby got in touch with Fritz Gerg, the President of the Federation of German Industry, and with Ulrich Lohmar and Walter Leisler-Kiep, two important members of the Bundestag (the West German Parliament). Lohmar tried to help; he told Nannen that a new German Press Law would be passed with tough restrictive clauses which would create grave problems for publishers who printed objectionable material about ex-members of foreign governments or their families.

Nannen also said that Bobby had tried to enlist Chancellor Kurt George Keisinger in his crusade to stop *Der Stern* from printing the *verboten* material. Keisinger, to his credit, wanted to know what kind of democracy would countenance such an action on his part.

Fritz Berg, the President of the Federation of German Industry, sent a letter to Nannen, in which he said that there would be a great deal of unpleasantness, especially about economic matters affecting the United States and Germany, if the editor persisted in his intentions to print the deleted material.

Bobby also contacted Kurt Birrenbach, an important West German politician, who asked the publisher to agree to the cuts. Bobby also sent telegrams to Bucheris and Nannen again raising the questions of the cuts, practically demanding that they be made.

"I didn't agree that those 1,600 words are of no political significance," Nannen said. "And *Stern* is not interested in helping a Senator from the United States to achieve his political ambitions at the expense of historical truth." The editor said that he was prepared to cut certain personal items but not the political ones. He insisted on including those passages that described Johnson's crude behavior and several paragraphs which pointed up that a state of war existed between the Kennedys and the Johnsons.

150

He stated his reasons for including the forbidden passages quite succinctly "because I'm certain that the book was Bobby Kennedy's original plan to lower Johnson's popularity by damaging his reputation, and I wanted that fact brought to light."

Nannen could see nothing unusual about Johnson's behavior on the plane trip back from the Dallas tragedy. Assuming the role of a sociologist, he explained that Johnson and the people who hailed from New England had different kind of mentalities. Johnson, he said, acted in accordance with his Texas upbringing. The New Englander's standard of values were radically different from the Texan's. It was true that Johnson's behavior had been crude. It was, he admitted, "clumsy and tasteless."

"I think the Kennedy family is trying to preserve Jackie as a national monument at least until Robert becomes President. Because they were opposed to her decision to move to New York with her friends and take part in the life of high society."

After the West German courts decided in favor of *Stern,* Nannen volunteered to delete 122 words because they were of a personal nature. He refused, however, to eliminate the political material. It was his opinion that Bobby had injured himself because of his becoming involved in the fight with Manchester.

Johnson did not fare much better. He evidently realized that he had been smudged. After the brawl had subsided, Drew Pearson published an article in the *Der Diezeit* magazine (published by Bucheris, the same owner of *Der Stern)* highly laudatory about Johnson. When Nannen asked Pearson if the President had inspired him to write the piece, the columnist admitted it was true. He said that he had first broached the idea to Johnson, who answered that it was an "excellent idea."

Publishing the article made it clear that Nannen and Bucheris were buttering up President Johnson, to appease him, for he was the real power in Washington, rather than support a man who *might* become a force.

The Manchester affair had left a residue of hatred and destruction among the principals. Bobby, in voicing his differences with Johnson's foreign policies, aggravated and further embittered his relations with the embattled President.

Chapter 28
On Foreign Policy

Bobby, whose main interest had always been foreign relations, now turned to the deepening Vietnam crisis, finding himself at odds with the President more and more.

The Fulbright Hearings had made the public aware there were important senators unable to go along with the Administration on the escalation of the war. Dean Rusk, testifying at the Senate Foreign Relations Committee, mouthed the same cliches he had been saying for years: Hanoi was invading a free and sovereign country, the Viet Cong was an instrument of Hanoi, Ho Chi Minh was a Red Chinese stooge, and the capital of China was "Peiping" instead of Peking for reasons he alone could explain.

General Maxwell Taylor, a former ambassador to Vietnam and an adviser on foreign affairs for two Presidents, accused the American critics of Administration policies of prolonging the war and letting the boys down, saying that the Communists "have not forgotten that the Vietnamese had won more in Paris than they had gained at Dien Bien Phu," concluding, sarcastically, that the Viet Cong were as lucky with Washington politicians.

Senator Morse took that statement as a "personal affront," stating that he had no intention of getting down into the gutter with him.

In his book on the Kennedy Administration, corroborating the *Newsweek* story, Taylor was reported to have said, "that Diem's own lack of popularity in the countryside was handicapping anti-guerrilla efforts." Nothing was done to start the program. Why do anything! The Administration was sold on Diem. Johnson, who went to Vietnam when he was Vice President, called Diem "the Churchill of Asia."

Jean Lacouture, a French expert on Vietnam, in his book *Vietnam Between Two Truces,* wrote: "In 1955, every opponent had been denounced [by Diem] as a left-over from the *feudal rebels* supported by the colonialists. After 1956, every opponent was called a Communist. At first the struggle was conducted by simple means; concentration camps... It was the dictatorship in the South that kindled the fire."

Johnson sent an assortment of diplomats scurrying all over the globe to bring his message of peace. The expeditions proved to be a rank failures, however. The *Wall Street Journal,* certainly no mouthpiece for way-out radicals, had the following to say about Johnson's peace circus: "Where, in all the trashing about, is the opportunity for the deep reflection the war urgently demands? It might be argued that the length of America's involvement had provided time for every conceivable analysis of strategies, objectives and probabilities. If, so, there is little evidence that the time had been effectively employed. Whether or not you agree with retired General Gavin and former Ambassador Kennan, they have a point in contending that the United States should hold where it is until it can decide what it wants to do. Some disadvantages of expansion have been well rehearsed by now, the mounting risk of war with China, the diminishing ability to handle troubles that may erupt elsewhere. In addition, it seems to us there are disadvantages pertaining to Vietnam alone.

"Since the Communists have thus far matched or overmatched each American force buildup they are presumably capable of continuing to do so. In that event, in the sense of a clear-cut victory or in the limited sense of causing the Communists to cease fire and come to the conference table is not possible.

"Moreover, if the war within Vietnam gets bigger and bigger and goes on and on, the likelihood grows that there may not be any Vietnam left worth anyone's having. The United States is fighting to save South Vietnam, but there is a limit to the destruction of the people and the property that can be tolerated before something gives; the government collapses or the people refuse to take it any longer."

Just at the time when important journals of public opinion began to find a lot of fault with Johnson's policy, Bobby walked in and started giving voice to his own doubts. On suggesting that the National Liberation Front be included in future negotiations, Bundy, Rusk, McNamara and Johnson himself all shot him down. Humphrey, who was running all over Southeast Asia, shouted that it would be like "putting the fox in the chicken coop... or an arsonist in a fire department." Senator Russell Long, and George Meany, also voiced sharp differences with the Kennedy position. But Bobby continued to advocate his policy, declaring that the country could follow three

alternatives:
1. Kill or repress the Viet Cong;
2. Turn the country over to them; or,
3. Admit them to a share of power and responsibility.

Bobby believed the third was the only sensible alternative, adding that "it may come through a single conference or by a slow, undramatic process of gradual accomodation. It will require enormous skill and political wisdom to find the point at which participation does not bring domination or internal conquest. We must be willing to face the uncertainties of election and the possibility of an eventual vote on re-unification... There must be international guarantees to back up agreement, good faith, and mutual self-interest. And we must insist that the political process go forward under the rigorous supervision of a trusted international body."

His declaration of independence from the Johnson foreign policy caused a split in Democratic Party ranks and served to widen the chasm between the two men: "I didn't expect all that initial reaction... Humphrey, Bundy, Ball, all about the fox in the chicken coop and all that," Bobby complained. After all, who did he have to fear? Bundy, who left the government to accept a job to run the Ford Foundation? Ball, who suddenly discovered he was unable to support his family on a State Department salary? Rusk, who was just another appointed official with no political power base? And Humphrey, who lost his power because of his pro-war stance? Bobby could disregard them all.

Looking beyond Vietnam, he had something to say about China policies, believing that "there are reasonable and responsible steps which [we] can take to raise the possibility of improved relations with China in the future." He said that the Vietnam War would call for a greater commitment of American forces and entail a dangerous risk of a general war with China and the Soviets: "It would lead, indeed already has led' thoughtless people to advocate the use of nuclear weapons which would involve all these things— commitment, risk, and the spreading of destruction in pursuit of a goal which is at best uncertain and at worse unattainable.

"This means simply that we will neither demand nor yield specific formal commitments before bargaining begins. In fact, both sides must come to any discussion with at least one basic condition; one irreducible demand; one point they will not yield. For the United States, it must not turn Vietnam over to the North. For the North Viets, it must be that they will accept a settlement which leaves in the South a hostile government dedicated to final physical destruction of all Communist elements, refusing economic cooperation with the North, depedendent upon continued presence of American military power.

"A negotiated settlement means that each side must concede matters that are important in order to preserve positions that are essential."

Bobby took stands on other issues; he proposed that the United States serve as a nuclear umbrella for countries agreeing to withdraw from the nuclear race: "You give us your right to acquire nuclear weapons and we will take care of you with ours."

But the Administration had its own ideas. Arthur Goldberg, in a speech at the United Nations, said that the government was not prepared to go that far. Washington was willing to go along with a program predicated on finding ways to prevent nuclear blackmail, but it would not mortgage its own security in return for any other government's promise to forswear the making of nuclear arms.

Bobby countered Goldberg's thesis and said "that such guarantees of protection would only apply to cases of nuclear aggression. Such an umbrella must not be divorced from and superior to the other policy aims of the nation involved."

Bobby had great faith in his country's altruism. He thought that the United States was morally, intellectually and militarily competent to look after the well-being of the entire world.

It was the Vietnam War that made Johnson appear like a Goldwater. And it was Bobby's opposition to the President's position that made people believe he was a left of center.

On February 19, 1966, Bobby proposed giving the Viet Cong and its political wing, the National Liberation Front, "a share of power and responsibility in any elected government backed by international guarantees." He thought that the Front "might be admitted through elections to an interim government before the elections."

On April 27, he criticized the Administration for not allowing any "sanctuary or elsewhere for the North Vietnamese planes." He also was critical about the sending of bombers and fighters over North Vietnam where, according to him, "they invite attacks by Communist planes and increase the danger of escalation of the conflict."

He viewed it the greatest concern the clashes over North Vietnam, thinking it was "neither prudent nor wise to take such risks of escalating the war" until some progress had been made towards achieving the stability that is essential for the successful prosecution of our efforts in the United Nations."

A few weeks after he made that statement, he added that South Vietnam is where "the war is being fought and in which or goals can be accomplished [and] no military action in North Vietnam or China can create or contribute to the creation of a viable political structure in South Vietnam without such a structure."

Johnson sizzled with rage. His anger reached gigantic proportions. With his heart condition, he had to contend with Bobby, on top of everything else.

On a trip to Europe, Bobby was quoted as having told a meeting of Oxford University students that "the next few weeks will be crucial and critical" for either peace or war, hinting that talks were currently going on and that Soviet Premier Aleksei N. Kosygin, the British, the Americans and the North Vietnamese were involved.

Back in Washington, asked to explain what he had meant about "secret negotiations," he said that he had been misinterpreted, that he was just referreing to the expected visit of the Soviet Premier, that he had never intended to convey there were secret talks taking place. However, he continued to emphasize that the next few weeks would be crucial and critical.

In Paris, Bobby said that France "has a vital and significant role" to perform in the attempt to find a "peaceful solution." He met with Maurice Couve de Murville, the Minister of the Asia Department of the Foreign Ministry, with Andre Maraux, the Minister of Culture, with Jean Chauvel, a retired diplomat who had retained his title of Ambassador, with Pierre Mendes-France, with Jean Lecaunet, the right of center politician, with Francois Mitterand, the leader of the left opposition, with Etienne Manach, an important official at the Foreign Office, with William van der Heuvel, and finally with John G. Dean, an American embassy official considered an expert on Vietnam because he had lived there for six years.

Bobby encountered considerable difficulty in following the conversation of those men, for he knew little if any French, and the interpreter didn't help much. He learned through an excited Dean that the French had received proposals from Ho Chi Minh that went far beyond anything the State Department had been told so far.

By now, Bobby had made a complete circle: from an approver of the Vietnam War to a seeker of peace. Four years earlier in Saigon, he said "We are going to win in Vietnam. We shall remain here until we do win... I think that the American people understand and fully support this struggle," praising Ngo Dinh Diem as a "brave and patriotic" leader. Now, he was calling for "negotiations with the Viet Cong" because he was worried about the bombing of North Vietnam. When a *Ramparts Magazine* editor wanted to know in what way Johnson's policy differed from his brother's, who had initially escalated the war, Bobby replied that "there is a contradiction between a counter-insurgency position and the policy Johnson is pursuing."

Bobby had hardly set foot on U.S. soil after his self-imposed mission abroad when he received an urgent request to visit Johnson at the White House. Rumors about peace feelers were spreading all over, making Johnson appear like a reluctant dragon in no hurry to lay his hands on the dove of peace. For this reason, the President was not in a very good mood.

When Bobby, Nichols Katzenbach, Walt Rostow and a number of other luminaries walked into the Oval Room (February 6, 1967), according to reports, Bobby and the President resorted to a number of invectives and profane remarks. In the confrontation, which lasted about 45 minutes, Johnson warned Bobby that "if you keep talking like this, you won't have a political future in this country in six months." Warming up to his subject, Johnson included all the doves who were opposed to his Vietnam policies. "In six months, all you doves will be destroyed." Becoming more emotional, he shouted, "The blood of American boys will be on your head."

When Bobby attempted to tell the President that he did not leak the story about "secret talks," that it had probably been the State Department, Johnson shouted, "It's your State Department, not mine." Katzenbach winced at that remark. Finally, Johnson closed: "I never want to hear your views on Vietnam again." In addition, he told Bobby he never wanted to see him again.

Allegedly, Bobby called Johnson a s.o.b., that he didn't "have to sit there and take that...".

Always concerned about his public image, Johnson believed that Bobby was making him appear like a super Goldwater. He told Bobby to inform the newspapers that the government had never received any meaningful peace feelers from Hanoi. Bobby, however, insisted on examining the confidential memorandas before doing so.

"I'm telling you that you can take my word for it." But Bobby did not trust the President.

When the reporters questioned Bobby about the confrontation, Bobby denied there had been any brawl. But they kept asking uncomfortable questions, wanting to know if he had called the President a s.o.b., which Bobby quickly denied. He also denied being threatened by Johnson. Asked if the President had predicted his political demise, Bobby refused to comment. When asked if the President had said that the blood of American boys would be on his conscience if he continued to harass him, Bobby replied: "Not in that context, but I don't want to talk about that."

Despite his brave words, he told the reporters that he had briefed the President about his trip and concluded by saying that "I never felt that I was the recipient of any peace feelers." He praised Johnson's attempts to conclude the war: "He is making a diligent effort to obtain peace."

Representative Rogers C. B. Morton, a Republican, criticised Bobby for taking on himself to serve as "a one-man State Department, touring the capitals of Europe... Such trips make it more difficult and politically uncomfortable to stand firm behind the President."

In the Senate, meanwhile, six Democrats, including Vance Hartke of Indianda, Clairborne Pell of Rhode Island, Wayne Morse of Oregon, Joseph S. Clarke of Pennsylvania, Ernest Gruening of Alaska, and George McGover of South Dakota, delivered speeches calling for a suspension in the bombing over North Vietnam.

Speaking to university students in Chicago, Bobby said that the country had no China policy except for "sweeping statements, pious hopes, grandiose commitments and reflective fears." He assured them that there was nothing personal in his critique of Johnson's "stewardship of the war. The President had inherited a situation that was very complex and has acted with courage."

The blood had hardly been washed from the battlefield of the Oval Room when Bobby again trained his big elephant gun at the President in a speech on the Senate floor wherein he called for a cessation of the bombing and declared if the United States was sincere in its desire to start negotiations, it would definitely have to agree to include all parties to the conflict in the discussions and to accept the possibility that South Vietnam might elect a left-wing government. He accused Johnson of asking for concessions from the North Vietnamese that were harder than those he had demanded a year ago. At this time, his brother Teddy got into the act, predicting that the party would lose the national election if Johnson were not to conclude the war by 1968.

Schlesinger said that the Administration had misrepresented Hanoi's peace gestures because it "does not consider negotiations advantageous at this time." But Ambassador

Goldberg said, "That is not true. We are ready for unconditional negotiations today."

Johnson was burning all over again. In an obvious reference to Bobby, he said that some people insisted on adopting an attitude that peace was preferable out of a "temporary lust for popularity." Humphrey explained that the two antagonists had a "difference of opinion over details... Bobby has never asked for a withdrawal from Vietnam, and has never broken with the President on the fundamental principles of involvement."

On April 27, 1966, Bobby said that it was "neither prudent nor wise to take such risks of escalating [the] war until some progress has been made towards achieving the stability that is essential for the successful prosecution of our efforts in the United Nations." Shortly after making that declaration, he elaborated on his views in a television interview, saying that as a result of the conflict "our own country is split." He also declared that there was a "decline in our own leadership in the world. I found it in Latin America, Africa and Europe." But when the interrogators asked him why he had voted in favor of Johnson's war budget, he said he "could not in good conscience vote against it as long as our boys are fighting there." He hinted that Kosygin and Pogorney had said that the North Vietnamese would have come to the negotiating table if the bombing were to stop during the Tet holiday. He still believed that we should "end the bombing and go to the negotiating table and test their sincerity... A year ago the North Vietnamese declared that they would not come to talk unless [we] accept their four points. Now they have withdrawn the four points and said they would go. So the situation has changed drastically and dramatically. I think the situation has altered and it projects a unique opportunity."

Journalist William H. White trained his cannons on Bobby: "You have placed yourself at the head of the Anti-Johnson forces." To which Bobby retorted that his "first responsibility was to the country and the citizens of the State of New York... [and my] loyalty... to the country rather than to the Democratic Party."

Taking note of the Air Force generals and other brass who were plugging for a war with China, Bobby said that "No military action in North Vietnam or China can create or contribute to the creation of a viable political situation in South Vietnam without such a structure. The efforts of our fighting men will be wasted. Extension of the war into China will not solve the political problems within South Vietnam. Whatever such escalation might be expected to achieve, it will not bring to the conference table Nguyen Cao Ky or Thich Tri Quang, the

Buddhist leader, who do not talk to one another."

Taking on Johnson was not enough. J. Edgar Hoover, the national icon, was next.

Caught red-handed in a number of wire-tapping incidents, Hoover tried to get himself off the hook by saying that Bobby had sanctioned the wire taps while he was Attorney General. Hoover made the accusation in a letter to Congressman H. R. Gross, a Republican from Iowa. Bobby learned of it while touring the Bedford-Stuyvesant section of Brooklyn, a black ghetto. When reporters questioned him, he referred them to his Washington office. The man in charge of his staff said that Hoover had been "misinformed" and then displayed a letter (written by Courtney A. Evans, an Assistant Director of the FBI and liaison man between Hoover and Bobby) which stated that Bobby had not been informed about electronic bugging because Hoover had general authority to install hidden microphones without specific authorization.

The Hoover letter addressed to Congressman Gross contained a different version. It said that during Bobby's term of office at the Justice Department, "he had displayed a great interest in pursuing such matters and while in different areas not only listened to the results of microphone surveillance but raised questions relative to obtaining better equipment. He was briefed frequently by an FBI official regarding such matters."

Hoover asked Gross to examine a document signed by Bobby, in which he had discussed the use of leased telephone lines in the operation of hidden microphones in security and major criminal cases.

On May 24, 1966, Bobby was questioned by reporters on an ABC television program, *Questions and Answers*. The newspapermen asked if he had "authorized the FBI wire taps of gamblers' telephones in Las Vegas in 1962 and 1963." Bobby denied sanctioning them: "[I have] never authorized wiretaps except in national security cases."

Bobby and Hoover were both lying. In 1961, Bobby sent a task force into Nevada to search for links between the gamblers and organized crime. The FBI, which had been using wire taps for years, found nothing objectionable about Bobby's request to listen in on the gamblers' conversations. As a matter of fact, they also checked on tax evasion by casino owners on behalf of the Bureau of Internal Revenue. They set up the Henderson Novelty Company in Las Vegas to serve as a blind to install 100 taps in the major casinos. One of the FBI agents later admitted that the office of Ruby Kalod, the propieter of the Stardust and

Desert Inn, had been wiretapped since 1963 to obtain evidence of *skimming*— taking money off the top and not declaring it in the income tax returns, and the diversion of funds for criminal activities.

Everyone in Las Vegas knew that the FBI and Bobby's men were violating state law but they kept silent about it until the 1966 elections. "Things were beginning to surface," as Bobby would say, and the gambling industry leaders in Nevada were demanding action. One politician said "The issue is, are we going to run our affairs without the interference of a government agency? And another said, "Appeasement is no more answer to federal invasion of state's rights than it was to Hitler."

Governor Sawyer called for the prosecution of the FBI for violation of the state laws, and Ed Marshall, Las Vegas' District Attorney, who was opposing Sawyer in the primaries, threatened to have a full scale Grand Jury investigation of the FBI actions. A special commission which had investigated the charges against the gamblers gave them a clean bill of health. When the FBI agents refused to appear for the commission hearings, Governor Sawyer charged the federal government with "blackmail, deceptions and deliberate violations of the law." He also accused the FBI of using Nazi-like tactics and of having run "roughshod over our state law and the United States Constitution."

The Justice Department was out to clear itself and put Hoover on the spot. A memo was sent to the Supreme Court on May 24, 1966 which stated that one, Fred B. Black Jr., a Washington public relations man, had been the subject of a tap by the FBI during the period of February 7 to April 25, 1964 in his hotel suite in the capital. Thurgood Marshall, the Solicitor General, said that Hoover "had approved the installation of a device in this case. Bobby, who had probably ordered that the memo be sent to the Supreme Court, said that he had not been informed about the tap.

A former FBI agent, by the name of Turner, has written several magazine articles exposing Hoover's use of taps to get evidence, and his deployment of agents to do "second story" work as well for the same purpose. And of course, Bobby had also been accused of using taps in the Hoffa case.

It all boiled down to the pot calling the kettle black. Both Hoover and Bobby had been using taps for years, but neither would own up to it in public.

Chapter 29
The Presidential Sweepstakes

In the spring of 1967, Allard Lowenstein, a young Long Island lawyer, who years later was to meet a tragic death at the hands of a long-time admirer, tried to persuade Bobby to run for the Presidency. During a plane trip to California, where both men were to attend a dinner for Jesse Unruh, the Kingpin of the state's Democrats. Lowenstein blueprinted his plan on how to dispose Johnson as President. He told Bobby that Johnson was going to suffer a humiliating defeat in the upcoming New Hampshire primary. It was the gospel truth, he said. The time was ripe for Bobby to plunge into the race, assuring him that the party would nominate him. Lowenstein also told Bobby that Unruh could probably be persuaded to run a peace slate of delegates in California. Bobby listened attentively, but made it quite clear that he was not ready to challenge Johnson, for he believed it would be an exercise in futility to declare himself a candidate.

"He took it as seriously as the idea of a parish priest disposing a Pope," Lowenstein said. "He was not quite ready to commit himself." He asked who might challenge Johnson, and Lowenstein gave the name of General Gavin, a registered Republican.

Lowenstein then thought to ask John Kenneth Galbraith (a leader of the Americans for Democratic Action, one who had been criticising Johnson's foreign policies especially from an economic point of view) to run for the Presidency, only to discover that he had been born in Canada and that his parents were Canadian citizens.

While Bobby was finding it difficult to make up his mind. Gene McCarthy announced his candidacy for the high office. And Bobby accepted an invitation to attend a conference of "Concerned Democrats."

Shortly after that meeting, the Kennedy men held their own series of conferences, the first by Van der Heuvel in his Central Park West apartment, which included Teddy, Salinger,

Sorensen, Dolan, Dutton and Goodwin, some of whom were not urging Bobby to run, especially Schlesinger and Goodwin. But the well-known gourmet, Pierre, concluded that Bobby should challenge Johnson. Sorensen, on the other hand, and as cautious as usual, also told him not to consider running.

Bobby should have known better than to take advice from the so-called experts. His late brother had learned the lesson the hard way over the Bay of Pigs disaster.

At the second session, Van der Heuvel, never considered a profound thinker, came up with an idea: Bobby should persuade Johnson to have him as his Vice President.

One of the advisors who had told him not to run said that Bobby's future was now hanging in the balance; if he announced his candidacy, Bobby would destroy the Democratic Party. Bobby showed little patience to that kind of gloom and doom.

"My future is not the issue. The issue is whether the country can survive four more years of Lyndon Johnson. If by declaring myself a candidate I could end the war sooner, I'd feel an obligation to run."

He asked himself many questions, the most important being, "How long should I keep on listening to these experts?"

Then Ted, just back from an inspection tour of Vietnam, told Bobby the corruption was rampant there, that it was a bottomless pit into which American men and money were being wasted.

Meanwhile, Ethel, with Bobby's younger political associates, needled him to take a stand once and for all against the advice of the older associates who were advising caution. With time marching on, Bobby knew he could not put off his announcement.

At a breakfast held at the National Press Club, political writers again asked the important questions. Although the session was off-the-record, when the inevitable question was raised, Bobby said that it would take "an act of God" to keep Johnson from being re-elected, adding that it had been Senator McCarthy of Minnesota who had started the rumors about his entering the race.

In a discussion with Euguene Salinger, Bobby produced a letter written by Pete Hamill, a young newspaperman and a dove. In it, Hamill poured out his pent-up distaste for Johnson as well as his disgust about the never-ending conflict in Vietnam, and begged Bobby to declare himself a candidate. Although the letter had made a deep impact on Bobby, he still hesitated, much as he did with his brother John over the Attorney General appointment. But when Goodwin threatened to go to New Hampshire to help McCarthy, Bobby finally decided to make a stand.

"This was one of the great disasters of all time for the United States," he said. "But Gene McCarthy hasn't been able to tap the unrest in the country. You have to be able to touch the uneasiness... It would be far more effective if McCarthy had been able to touch that spirit if he went to what really troubles them rather than getting on as he did speaking about the war and being a sort of peace candidate."

The Tet military offensive made the American people aware that the Pentagon had been indulging in wishful thinking by assuring everyone that the enemy was about to be destroyed.

Knowing that Johnson had no intention of calling off his misadventure in Southeast Asia, and with the unfolding of the Tet offensive, Bobby finally decided to run for the Presidency, declaring himself a candidate on the eve of McCarthy's victory in the New Hampshire primary.

Ted, the loyal brother, declared that Bobby had discussed the situation with him and decided to become an active candidate five days before the New Hampshire primary.

"I was supposed to tell Gene that Bob was considering running," Ted said. "There was some question of whether I would be the best one to tell him. I mentioned the possibility to Goodwin about talking to him."

While that activity was going on, Johnson announced he was *not* running. Bobby did not hear the news, as he was on a plane bound for New York.

"The President is not going to run," yelled John Burns when the plane landed. Bobby was speechless for a few moments, unable to comprehend what Burns was saying. Burns had to repeat the statement several times before Bobby finally reacted.

On walking down the ramp, Bobby found a large group of men and women standing nearby, shouting, "You're the next President."

At home, Ethel, as lively as ever and clad in a short black and white dress, served drinks to Bobby's aides. While Sorensen began to compose a statement, Bobby walked into the bedroom to telephone Ted.

The campaign was in high gear. In Washington, President Johnson could now indulge in some dramatics of his own. He hastened to assure Bobby that he was only the caretaker of the

Kennedy Administration, that he attempted to raise the moral standard of the American people: "I hope he'll look down and say I did the right thing and fulfilled what he would have wanted me to do for the stockholders."

If one didn't know better, Johnson's oration would have sounded convincing. He had never been an admirer of any of the Kennedys. He had doubts about Bobby's mental abilities, and always commented about his lack of experience. Furthermore, Johnson never thought that his Administration was an extension of that of John F. Kennedy. He loved power for its own sake and enjoyed exercising it, profoundly irritated with Bobby's constant reminders that he was only an "accidental" President.

Bobby listened to Johnson, not believing for one moment that the Texan would keep his hands off the oncoming election campaign. Humphrey, who had been Bobby's faithful servitor, would be appropriately rewarded. However, He knew he had a great deal to fear from Johnson, who would do anything to win the nomination for Humphrey. There was also Gene McCarthy, and his suporters still criticized by Bobby for his attempts to snatch the party's nomination.

Bobby now had a more serious problem on his hands. Don Dillinger, the political director of the Machinist Union and a Bobby supporter, said that the labor leaders "felt strongly about Bobby... [but] couldn't quite explain why they had so instinctive a dislike for the man... there were the standard reasons— the persecution of Hoffa and his attitude towards wiretapping. There was something irrational about it all."

The business people had their questions too. Hobart Rowen, the financial editor of the *Washington Post*, said that they "hated him instinctively. They hated *Jack* too, but they hated Bobby more— an attitude difficult to understand because basically Bobby's ideas on fiscal matters were conservative. Both he and Jack stood for policies that were good for business, but business hated them both."

In a poll of 160 important business executives, only three favored Bobby. Many said the he wasn't "safe" for the country; others felt that he had made it quite evident that he was unfriendly towards business as demonstrated during the steel crisis in 1962, from which it has yet to recuperate; a few accused him of having no understanding of economics.

One Wall Street mogul thought Bobby "power-hungry, overly-ambitious and over-sexed." To be fair, Bobby never displayed the latter characteristic in public.

The primaries quickly took on a vigorous tone between Bobby and Gene McCarthy. Bobby's first hurdle came in Indiana, a conservative state and a hot-bed of Ku Klux Klan followers. A liberal politician was certain to face a difficult time trying to persuade the voters that he was *not* a dangerous man. In that state, Nixon had scored a victory over John F. Kennedy with a majority of 250,000 votes in the 1960 national election. When Bobby arrived in Terre Haute, he was greeted with disparaging signs, such as "Coon Catcher," etc. Another suggested that he should be "defoliated." None intimidated him, however.

"The poor are hidden in society," he said. "No one sees them anymore. They are small minority in a rich country. Yet, I am stunned by the lack of awareness of the rest of Americans towards them and their problems. We don't see them. We pay all these taxes and pass all these programs, and yet the programs don't reach them and the taxes go for other things. And every year their lives are more hopeless than ever, and yet we wonder what is wrong with them."

In Gary, the blacks were out in full force giving him a very enthusiastic reception; the whites, however, were hostile. During the recent election for mayor, local Democrats attempted to steal votes from Hatcher, a black candidate. Richard Tuck, one of Bobby's associates, had been sent to Gary to put a halt to the frauds, knowing that the voting machines were either tampered with, or they would break down conveniently on election day. Bobby arranged for a number of black pinball repairmen to work on model voting machines, so that when on election day the machines broke down, the repairmen would be immediately dispatched. Hatcher was elected, thanks to Tuck and Bobby.

In the Nebraska primary, McCarthy told an audience in Omaha that the Kennedys were "poisoning the well in Indiana." Angry over Bobby's late arrival in the Presidential sweepstakes, Gene, nevertheless, did not wage a strong campaign in Nebraska, or elsewhere for that matter, for the simple reason that he just did not seem to have the temperament of a President.

Bobby decided to throw the gauntlet to McCarthy by asking him to debate the issues in California which contained all the diverse elements of the national electorate. It was the first primary with the three leading contenders facing each other. According to Bobby, the results would indicate what the country wanted, and he promised to withdraw from the race if he lost.

Before debating, he toured Los Angeles where immense crowds of blacks, and Mexican Americans stood in the streets to cheer him on. He made speeches in the main sectors of the city. Rafer Johnson, the black Olympic decathlon champion, accompanied him. Hundreds of hands reached up to touch Bobby as he passed by. When he asked their help, they all roared with approval, assuring him of their support. He made no bones about voicing his distaste for Mayor Yorty, an anti-Kennedy politician from way back. It was Yorty, as was later revealed, who ordered the police to warn the people to "get off the streets. You'll get hurt," thus reducing the size of the Kennedy crowds.

While Bobby was busy reaping a harvest of votes, McCarthy was gleaning the fields in San Francisco. At Stockton, he chastised Bobby: "There is a line of poetry about 'summer patriots.' There should be something about spring and summer patriots. They should have been with me in New Hamsphire."

He accused Bobby of having supported Johnson's intervention in the Dominican Republic, which was not true. On the other hand, Bobby had never faulted the U.S. Government when it sent warships to encourage the overthrow of the Goulart Regime in Brazil; he also went along with the establishment of Counter-Intelligence groups to promote order around the globe (an euphemism for subverting unfriendly governments), for which he could have been criticised but was not.

In their television debate, Bobby orated on the need to alleviate the plight of the underprivileged: "We can fight for freedom 2,500 miles away. But we must do something to deal with the quality of life here. The property taxes for the people in the cities is too overbearing."

The suburbanites found MacCarthy's aloofness to their liking, respecting his supposed intellectual approach and his quiet demeanor. They disliked Bobby for the opposite reasons. Nominations, however, are not won by appealing exclusively to a candidate's attributes, or to the middle class. McCarthy may not have attached too much importance to winning the minority groups, and the blue collar workers, but his staff did, for the simple reason that they may have understood that number-wise those so called *minorities*, vote wise, may have the Los Angeles majority. As a result, they planned a barbacue in the Watts area, a "restless" black ghetto.

It was quite a scene to see McCarthy's futile attempt to speak while the people devoured the food as though there was no tomorrow. "There's never been a group in America who had anymore reason to organize themselves to get their rights than 'he blacks," Gene said, his words falling on deaf ears.

When McCarthy said that the black masses should get out

of their ghettos and move into government housing in the suburbs where the jobs were to be found, Bobby reiterated that that made no sense at all. Instead, he said that, "I am in favor of moving people out of their ghetto, but we have 14 million Negroes here in the ghetto at the present time. We have here in the state of California a million Mexican Americans whose poverty is even greater than any of the black people's. I mean, when you say you are going to take 10,000 black people and move them into Orange County... take them out where 40% of them don't have jobs at all, that's what you are talking about. But if you are talking about hitting the problem in a major way—taking those people out, putting them into the suburbs where they can't afford the housing, where their children can't keep up with the schools, and where they don't have the schools for the jobs it's going to be catastrophic. I don't want to have them moved. Other groups have moved in the United States as they got the jobs and got the training. They moved themselves into the other areas of the United States and were accepted.

"They will find jobs and employment. but that does not exist, that's not the conditions that we are facing in this country at the present time."

Bobby insisted that no sane person could contemplate moving people out of ghetto in a year or two or three. It would take several decades before the exodus would become a reality. That kind of advice was bound to appeal to the residents of reactionary Orange County.

A day or so after the confrontation, McCarthy took up the matter of a mass exodus of Negroes into Orange County. He said that his opponent was trying to "frighten" the citizens there, and that his own views on the problem had been misinterpreted by Bobby.

In the past months, he said, "I have proposed programs to enable the Negroes to express the oppressive conditions in the ghetto and find better lives for themselves outside the inner city, in the beltline and beyond, where most of the new jobs are." He concluded by stating that Bobby was beginning to sound like then California Governor Ronald Reagan.

The day before the election, Bobby was bone tired, yet there were other places to go and other people to see. He flew from Los Angeles to San Francisco where he addressed various groups, and took part in a motorcade to Long Beach. Then he joined another motorcade en-route to San Diego, and afterwards flew back to Los Angeles.

In San Diego, he addressed a large outpouring of people at the El Corez Hotel auditorium where his good friend, Andy

Williams, sang. No one knew, however, that Bobby had had a weak spell before going on stage, and had to be taken to the dressing room where he retched up the remains of the ginger ale he had been drinking all day, as Rafer Johnson and Bill Brier stood guard while the candidate recovered from his temporary indispostion.

The last of his alloted time on earth, Bobby spent in relaxing from the weary rounds of campaigning. He stayed at the home of John Frankenheimer, the television and motion picture director, where he slept until 11 A.M. After a leisurely lunch with his wife and six children, he took the family to the beach. Although it was cloudy and the water was cold, Bobby could not resist taking a quick dip. With his son, David, swimming alongside, they raced each other. When David got caught in an undertow, Bobby quickly swam over and managed to catch him and drag him out of the water to safety. As he stood over his son, for a few long and deep moments, Bobby stared into the blue eyes of the young boy, much as his brother Joe Jr. had done when he jumped off the boat and almost drowned.

In the late afternoon, the family went back to the Frankenheimer home where Bobby took a brief rest before leaving for the Ambassador Hotel. Ethel was not ready, and he went without her.

Upon arrival at the hotel, he took the elevator to the Royal Suite, which served as his campaign headquarters. It was jammed with many local luminaries and campaign workers as well as reporters and others who served themselves drinks from the well-stocked bar.

Accompanied by Dutton and Frankenheimer, Bobby walked into the lobby to a rousing welcome. Then the three went to the suite where Sorensen, Goodwin, Jesse Unruh, Pat Lawford and Stephen and Jean Smith were waiting together with the unpredictable Jimmy Breslin.

Dutton telephoned in South Dakota to learn that Bobby was winning. In Minnesota, Bobby had received 49.8% of the vote to Johnson's 2% and to McCarthy's 9%. Gratified, Bobby insisted on calling Bill Dougerty, his campaign manager, to express his appreciation.

The reports of the California primary started to trickle in towards 8 P.M. McCarthy showed 49% of the vote to Bobby's 40%. Later, these figures were going to change dramatically.

While Bobby conferred with his aides, McCarthy was interviewed by David Schoumacher. Sensing defeat, McCarthy downgraded the importance of that disappointment: "We made our real test in Oregon where there were no minority blocs to destroy the results as in California," implying that it was no great feat for a Democrat to win over the minorities at a time when Nixon was the Republican nominee. He stressed that most of the independent vote was in his corner and that in the last analysis it was each bloc that was the key to victory in the November elections. In Oregon, Gene admitted he had appealed to the "educated people."

Bobby hesitated to appear on television while the results were still inconclusive, although indications had him the winner. He attempted to beg off, but was finally persuaded by well-wishers that he should address the nation. Although the votes from Los Angeles began to trickle in, he was still running 8% behind McCarthy. Finally, on seeing he *was* winning, he appeared on television and asked Gene McCarthy and his supporters to align themselves with him. Together, he assured the audience, they would defeat the establishment. After the appearance, he walked back to his suite where CBS's Roger Mudd interviewed him. Again Bobby called for McCarthy to support him. "Together we will be able to defeat Humphrey... perhaps we could unite now that the primaries are finished... and try to accomplish what we all started out to accomplish, which was for the cause, for a purpose, not for an individual."

When Mudd told him that he was "not going to be able to shake McCarthy," Bobby said that it was "really up to him. I mean, he's going to have to make that decision himself."

A tough questioner, Mudd commented on Humphrey's candidacy: "You have no way now between California and Chicago to draw the Vice Presidency into a fight."

"I don't think that the policies that he espoused would be successful in the country and I don't think they'd be successful with the Democratic Party, and I think all the primaries have indicated that," Bobby replied.

Mudd wouldn't let up: "Are you saying, Senator, that if the Democratic Party nominates the Vice President it will be cutting its own throat in November?"

"Well," Bobby began in an uncomfortable tone, "again you use those expressions. I think that the Democratic Party would be making a very bad mistake to ignore the wishes of the people and ignore the primaries."

Bobby then met with Robert Clark and with Dan Blackburn of *Metromedia News*. At this time, Mankiewicz informed Bobby that his supporters were clamoring to see him in the hotel's Embassy Room. As he was about to leave, Unruh and some NBC newscasters informed him that he had indeed won the California primary.

In discussing with Dutton and Mankiewicz what to say to his supporters, they suggested that Bobby talk about his victories in South Dakota and California, and that he should make a point of emphasizing that the results clearly showed that the victories had proved that everyone, including the farmers and the urban masses, favored his candidacy. Bobby told Goodwin to call Allard Lowenstein in New York alerting him to standby for a call.

At precisely 11:45 P.M., Bobby took the service elevator to the main ballroom, by way of the kitchen. Walking through, he paused to acknowledge the cheers from the domestics. Then he hurried through a dimly lit corridor to the Embassy Room where hundreds of his partisans were waiting impatiently.

The band began to play a campaign song. On seeing Ethel, who had just arrived, Bobby walked over to her. Dressed in an orange and white mini-dress with white stockings, she then accompanied Bobby to the platform amidst the cheering crowd.

He mentioned Don Drysdale, the star Los Angeles pitcher, taking note that he had broken a Major League record. "He pitched his sixth straight shutout tonight, and I hope that we have as good fortune in our campaign."

He expressed his gratitude to his brother-in-law for the superb manner in which he directed the primary, and praised Cesar Chavez, the leader of the striking grape pickers, Jesse Unruh, the Democratic High Lama, Paul Schrade, a local official of the United Auto Workers Union, Rafer Johnson, and Rosey Grier, the gigantic tackle of the Los Angeles Rams— men who, in a large measure, were responsible for victory. He told the voters that the football hero had promised to "take care of anyone who didn't vote for me." Further, he expressed his appreciation for the devotion that his dog Freckles had shown toward him, and gave special praise to his wife Ethel. Then he talked about the farmers of California and South Dakota: "Here is [California] the most urban state of any of the states in our Union, [and] South Dakota the most rural of any of the states in our Union. We were able to win in both. I think that we can end the divisions within the United States.

"What I think is quite clear is that we can work together in the last analysis, and that what has been going on within the United States over a period of the last three years— the division, the violence, the disenchantment with our society, the divisions whether it's between blacks and whites, will be ended."

171

After the speech, he was asked to address another group, but Dutton said that it made no sense as that group had already heard Bobby on closed-circuit television. One of his staff suggested that Bobby go to a room reserved for the press, located just beyond the corridor. Dutton and another friend had expected to lead him though that corridor. When they saw Bobby, who had unexpectedly jumped off the platform to be guided by Karl Eucker, the assistant maitre d'hotel, through the hallway, Dutton immediately ran after him.

Standing unnoticed near an ice machine in the kitchen was a man with a gun in his hand. As Bobby walked into the kitchen with Ethel following, some of the employees tried to shake his hand. Nearby, the members of his entourage looked on. At 12:13 A.M., just as Bobby was responding to a question on how he intended to campaign against Humphrey, a series of shots reverberated through the room. He stumbled to the floor, fatally wounded.

The gunman was still firing his revolver when writer George Plimpton, and Jack Gallican, a Kennedy aide, seized him. Assisted by Uecker, Eddy Minasian, Rosey Grier and Rafer Johnson, after a lot of scuffling, they were able to force the assassin to the floor. On pulling the gun out of his hands, Johnson began to shout, "Why did you do it, why?"

"I can explain," the gunman wimpered. "Let me explain!"

Karl Uecker, who was standing in front of Bobby, later described the scene: "I'm right in front of him. There were four shots, one after the other.

"The assassin was standing near a corner of the worktable in the kitchen passageway. He looked like a houseman. I did not know that the Senator had been hit. The first or second shot hit him. I wrestled with the gunman. I thought it was a joke or something. It sounded like Chinese firecrackers or something. I had my hand on the Senator. I was leading him and his wife..."

Transformed into a mob, the crowd was bent on a lynching. "You bastard, you'll fry for this," shouted one man. A woman screamed, "Oh God, it can't happen to this family again!"

Bobby lay on the cement floor. A priest bent over him to administer the last rites. A man suddenly shoved him aside: "He doesn't need a priest; he needs a doctor."

Pandemonium reigning, many demanded that the assassin be killed on the spot, while others demanded that he not be harmed. As news photographers aimed their flashing cameras on Bobby, Unruh grabbed one very rude photographer and punched him in the face. Ethel, who had been pushed back to safety, was now struggling to get back to her husband. As she

172

moved forward, a young man made caustic and insulting remarks about all politicians, including Bobby.

"Don't talk that way about the Senator," Ethel cried.

"Lady, I've been shot," he answered.

Ethel knelt down and kissed the 17-year old Edward Stroll. She then quickly made her way to Bobby. She knelt by his side and whispered to him, touching his hands which clutched a string of rosary beeds. When the crowd pressed on the stricken leader, Dick Tuck blew a whistle, urging them to move away, which they did. Someone placed an icepack on Bobby's forehead; another made a makeshift pillow out of a jacket and placed it under his head. Yet another loosened Bobby's tie and opened his shirt; then removed the shoes.

Hays Gorey, a magazine writer, noticed that Bobby's "lips were slightly parted, the lower one curled downwards, as it often was. Bobby seemed aware. His eyes seemed almost to say, 'So this is it.'"

In the Embassy Room, Stephen Smith cleared the room. A few minutes later, a physician appeared together with more policemen who took the killer from Rafer and Rosey. The officers began to clear a path to the street, but it was like rushing through an Indian gauntlet. Jesse Unruh, who knew that the crowd was bent on killing the assassin, kept on shouting, "I want him alive; keep him alive!"

Others who were wounded were taken to a nearby hospital. They were Paul Schrade, severly wounded in the head, Ira Goldstein, hit in his left lip, William Weisal, wounded in his abdomen, Elizabeth Evans, and the boy, Edward Stroll.

Bobby was taken to the Central Receiving Hospital where the doctors immediately gave him a cardiac massage and an injection of adrenalin. A news photographer attempted to crash his way into the emergency room to take a picture of the dying leader. On seeing the intruder bursting forth, Bill Barry pushed him aside with a slug to the face. Ethel and the priest, meanwhile, were having a hard time getting by the guard. Ethel ordered him to stand aside. Instead, he displayed his badge. She slapped it out of his hand. He lunged at her hitting her on the chest.

Standing next to Father Thomas Peacho of St. Basil's Church, Ethel watched the priest administer Extreme Unction.

Bobby was then taken to the Good Samaritan Hospital. On the way, the ambulance attendees administered plasma and dextrose. Ethel, Pat Lawford, Dave Hacket and Jean and Stephen Smith followed prayerfully.

In the emergency room, the doctors analyzed the three

wounds: the first a superficial one, the second and the third very severe. The hollow-nosed slugs had scattered into pieces when they came in contact with the bones.

For almost four hours, the doctors probed away trying to remove the fragments, to no avail.

The Senator, who had lived in so many parts of America and represented so many Americans— the *national* Senator was doomed.

Meanwhile, the "suspect," Sirhan Sirhan, a Jordanian nationalist, was taken to the North Los Angeles Police Headquarters. Police Chief Thomas Redkin, determined not to have a repeat of the Dallas incident when Jack Ruby gunned down Harvey Oswald, used a patrolman's pickup truck to take the surly assassin to the Hall of Justice where a hastily summoned judge presided over the procedings. Public Defender Richard Buckley, acting on behalf of the defendant, looked on as the Jordanian was charged with six counts of assault with intent to murder.

Sirhan was then taken to a windowless maximum-security cell in the hospital part of the Central Jail for Men. A guard was stationed in the cell and another keept watch from an aperture in the door. Outside, 100 armed guards patrolled the jail.

The police at first were not aware of Sirhan's true identity. They saw a small, dark-complexioned man, barely over five feet tall, brown eyes, thick, black hair, who spoke English with a distinct foreign accent, and not much more. His fingerprints showed no prior record. The Chief thought Sirhan was either a Cuban or a West Indian because Sirhan did not have any identifying papers. He did have four 100 dollar bills, one five dollar, four one dollar bills and small change. He also had a car key in his jacket and a newspaper column by David Lawrence, a conservative journalist, who had written that Kennedy was a dove on the Vietnam War and a strong supporter of Israel.

The police questioned the prisoner over and over, but Sirhan refused to respond, preferring to "remain incomunicado." According to the police, he was "very cool, very calm, very stable, and very lucid." Then unexpectedly, the "very cool" murderer changed his mind and decided to talk— not about his attempt to murder Kennedy, but about details of a Los Angeles murder case. "I want to ask questions," he said blazenly. "Why don't you answer *my* questions?"

He spoke about the stock market and gave the officers a summation of an article he had read about Hawaii. He spoke about his love of gardening and said that criminal justice tends to discriminate against the poor. When he saw that the police were not treating him as an equal, he told them, "I am not a mendicant." He spoke about everything under the sun; yet he refused to give his name to the police. After hours of interrogation, he asked for something to eat. He was fed a breakfast of eggs and sausage.

While the police were attempting to have Sirhan reveal who he was, other officers were trying to find out where he had bought the gun, a snub-nosed Iver-Johnson 8-shot revolver, Model 55 Sa. costing only $32.95. Through its serial number, the police learned that it had been registered with the State Criminal Identification and Investigation Bureau, and that its original owner was Albert L. Hertz of Alhambra. He had purchased the gun supposedly as a safety measure during the Watts riots of 1965. When the police contacted Hertz, he said that he had given the gun to his daughter, Mrs. Robert Westlake of Pasadena. She, in turn, gave it to George Erhart, an 18-year old youth, who in turn sold it to Joe Erhart, a bushy-haired department store employee who turned out to be Munir (Joe) Sirhan, 20 years old, an employee of Nash Department Store.

The background of the gunman was an "open book." Sirhans's family had resided in Jerusalem where his father, Bishara Salameh Sirhan, was employed at the local waterworks, but had lost the job after Palestine had been partitioned. According to those who knew him, the old man was a tyrant. His mother, on the other hand, was very religious. At one time, she applied for an expense-free passage to the United States with money provided by the United Nations Relief and Welfare Agency. The father, unable to adjust to the new country, returned to Jordan where he bought an olive grove.

A magazine writer who interviewed the elder Sirhan at his home in Taiyiba reported him as having said that he did not approve of his son nor of his deed: "I don't know how this happened and I don't know who pushed him to do this. I raised him to love. I tell you frankly: now I am against him."

Sirhan's neighbors in Los Angeles found it difficult to believe that the "nice, quiet young man" had shot the Senator. Residents in the area where he lived said that he was "nice, thoughtful and helpful." He liked to talk about books and played Chinese checkers with the older women— one of whom was Jewish.

An unemployed school dropout, Sirhan Sirhan made a point of telling everyone that he was an alien, contending that the "Jews had everything but still used violence to get pieces of

Jordan land."

It was now evident that he disliked all politicians who supported Israel, although local politicians kept that fact from the public. Evelle Younger, the District Attorney, and Thomas Lynch, State Attorney General, concurred with that decision. Believing that the public should know, Mayor Yorty revealed the contents of Sirhan's diary during a press conference, reporting that Sirhan had written that Bobby must be killed before the Fifth of June— the first anniversary of the 1967 Arab-Israeli War, that Gamal Abdel Nasser of Egypt was a great hero. Yorty further reported that Sirhan was a pro-Communist and an anti-American alien, one who consorted with dangerous bands of extremists.

In this new role as public prosecutor, jury and judge, Yorty made life difficult for the authorities, which didn't much concern him. He was concerned about making political gains for himself.

The police, however, were more circumspect. They informed Sirhan that he had the right of counsel and told him that he did not have to respond to their questions. They contacted the local office of the American Civil Liberties Union and suggested that a lawyer be assigned to represent the accused.

While Yorty was doing his best to mine political gold, the *national* Senator was breathing his last moments of life in the intensive care unit of the hospital.

In New York City, meanwhile, Jacqueline was awakened by the telephone. Her brother-in-law, Prince Radziwill, was calling from England. Having gone to bed early, she did not know about the tragedy. "You heard that he won in California," she joyfully announced.

"Yes," he answered, "but how is he?"

"I just told you. He won in California."

After the Prince told her that Bobby had been shot, she quickly dressed and flew to Los Angeles.

It was 4:45 A.M. The eyes of the world focused on the hospital. Press representative Mankiewicz appeared on the street. With a police microphone, he tried to make an announcement. Discovering the microphone wasn't working, he climbed up to the roof of the police car and shouted: "The doctors now say that the surgery will take another hour or perhaps two." He told reporters that Bobby's life signs— the heartbeat, respiration, blood pressure etc.— were good. He jumped from the car and walked into the hospital, his face sad and drawn. At 7:20 A.M., the doctors were still working feverishly to save Bobby's life, having removed all the fragments lodged in the brain except for a minute-size one which the surgeons did not "regard ... a major problem."

By evening, however, the doctors knew the end was near. Other endeavors were futile. Although the heart was beating, the machine recording the condition of Bobby's brain indicating it had for all practical purposes ceased to function. The end finally came.

With his head down, Mankiewicz walked into the press room, and in a voice that cracked under the strain, told the waiting reporters: "I have a short announcement to read at this time. 'Senator Robert Francis Kennedy died at 1:44 A.M. today, June 6, 1968. With him at the time of his death were his wife Ethel, his sisters, Mrs. Stephen Smith and Patricia Lawford, his brother-in-law Stephen and Mrs. John F. Kennedy. He was forty-two years old...' " Mankiewicz forgot to mention that Ted Kennedy was also present.

CHAPTER 30
The Investigation

Murdering Presidents and similar personalities has become a traditional practice in our violence-prone country.

A neurotic actor assassinated President Lincoln. There were the murders of Presidents James Garfield, William McKinley, and that of John F. Kennedy. There were also the attempted murders of Theodore Roosevelt, who carried the bullets in his body for the rest of his life, of Franklin Delano Roosevelt, of Harry S. Truman, of Gerald Ford, and of Ronald Reagan.

There were the murders of Robert F. Kennedy, of Dr. Martin Luther King, and the near-killing of Governor George Wallace of Alabama.

There are people who believe that Ted Kennedy's plane crash and the Chappaquidic incident may not have been accidents at all.

The bodies of President Kennedy and of Dr. King had hardly been interned when suspicions arose about conspiracies involving powerful men. Many also voiced suspicion that Bobby had been a target of conspirators who viewed his possible ascendancy to the Presidency with alarm.

Sirhan Sirhan was found guilty as charged. But shortly thereafter, questions were being asked. Things were not as they seemed to be. Among those to question the one-gun theory— the weapon used by Sirhan to kill Bobby— was the late Allard Lowenstein, a close friend and confidant of Bobby. There was also William W. Harper, famed criminologist. He raised embarrassing questions about the methods used by the police to determine who had committed the murder, and pointed out several discrepancies in the official version of the crime.

A number of witnesses noticed Sirhan dart about three or four feet in front of Bobby with his arm extended straight ahead, holding a .22 caliber revolver, and firing first around Uecker, who was escorting Bobby through the pantry, and then at Bobby Kennedy.

Harper believed that one of the three bullets was *not* fired by the Jordanian.

The clue that galvanized Lowenstein's theory was given in the report of Dr. Thomas T. Noguchi, the well-known Los Angeles coroner. He said that the powder burns proved quite clearly that Bobby had received the shot from behind at point blank range— about three inches, and possibly less. Noguchi spotted the inch-long "tattoo" of grayish sooty powder on the back edge of Bobby's ear, about an inch from the fatal head wound. It had penetrated slightly upward through the mastoid bone. He also discovered powder particles in the wound entrance itself and noted, on page 16 of his report, "Entry of gunshot wound is consistent with very close range of shooting. The powder residue indicated that the victim was shot at point-blank range."

Noguchi pointed this out before the grand jury. When asked by the Deputy District Attorney John Miner what "the maximum distance the gun could have been from the Senator and still have left some powder burns," Noguchi replied:

"Allowing for variation to be clarified by laboratory gun tests, I don't think it will be more than two or three inches from the edge of the right ear."

Uecker was asked, "How far was the suspect from Senator Kennedy and yourself at the time the first shot took place.?"

"How far?" he repeated. "As far as my left hand can reach... The maitre D's left hand had clutched the murdered man's right wrist as he was guiding him through the pantry. He had not let go of it until the second shot was fired."

Edward Minasian, a waiter, said that Sirhan's gun muzzle was about "three feet" from Bobby.

Edward DiPierro, a student, testified that Sirhan was four to six feet from Kennedy.

Other eye witnesses maintained that a second gun was used, insisting that while Sirhan shot at the Senator, another gunman hidden in the pantry pumped the fatal bullets; that it was impossible for Sirhan to have inflicted point-blank powder burns.

Evelle Younger pondered the conflicting stories, but did not voice his doubts in public. On May 13, 1974, however, he expressed his reservations.

Coroner Baxter Ward, a member of the County Board of Supervisors, also conducted an open hearing on the ballistics issue. He asked whether the District Attorney and Noguchi were aware of the conflicting facts. Noguchi said that, "One of the deputy district attorneys approached me after I testified before the Grand Jury on June 7, 1968 after having my testimony already transcribed, if I mis-stated, this is the time now to correct it, but I then told them that I don't have to be concerned about witnesses because I based my opinion totally on physical evidence...

"His reaction seemed to be, he was surprised that there was such a distance we were talking about."

Because Noguchi did not take the hints to cooperate with the politicians, they started to smear in public. In August 1968, the coroner's office was accused of "deficiencies" for the many "undetected" murders and "mislabeled" suicides—unjust accusations against a man of impeccable reputation, an expert who had conducted 4,000 autopsies in his eight years as coroner.

Attacks were also made on Noguchi's "flamboyant" personality, alleging that he made the following remarks: "I hope he dies because if he dies then my international reputation will be established."

He was to be called to testify at Sirhan's trial scheduled to begin on February 26, 1969. Three days before, supervisors leaked word that the coroner's alleged sins would be "ouster" hearings on February 25. With the heat on, everyone surmised that Noguchi would be forced to resign. Far from being intimidated, he took the stand and gave more or less the same facts, stating that additional gun tests had made him realize that his original estimate of the distance of the gun from the victim should be reduced at least 50%." He also said that the two back wounds which were close together in the right axille (armpit) had been inflicted at similarly "very close" range. Deputy District Attorney Lyn Compton asked Noguchi another question:

"When you say 'very close', what did you mean?"

"When I say 'very close', we are talking about the term of either contact or a half inch or one inch in distance."

Three weeks later, midway through Sirhan's trial, Noguchi was forced to resign on charges that he used amphetamins and barbiturates to excess and behaved "erratically and irrationally."

Five months later, he was reinstated by the County Civil Service Commission, sanitized of all alleged misconduct.

During the trial, David Fitts, Deputy District Attorney, produced Wayne Woler, chief of the Los angeles Police Crime Lab, who had supervised the muzzle-distance gun tests on June 11, 1968, five days after Noguchi had conducted his autopsy. Fitts told the jurors that the test firings were done with the weapon "recovered from the defendant." But Fitts referred to Sirhan's .22 caliber Iver Johnson revolver, serial # H53725 which Grier and Johnson had pulled out of the accused killer's hand. Wolfer, for some unexplained reason, used for the muzzle-distance tests a different Iver Johnson .22 serial # H18206 that had been signed out from the Property Clerk's office.

"Well," Wolfer testified, "I would say three-quarters of an inch. I really feel it was closer than an inch, but I gave you the maximum difference of an inch. I would say three-quarters of an inch at the inch distance than they did."

"When you use the word 'tolerance', are you saying that you added a quarter of an inch onto what your real opinion is?" asked Fitts.

"I would say I added possibly three-quarters of an inch."

"Well, that would be what in adding everything together, would that make an inch and three-quarters?"

"An inch."

"An inch?"

"Right!" answered Wolfer.

The newspapers now had a number of options. They had reported that Wolfer had said that the bullet was fired "approximately one inch" from Bobby's head, and the other two shots were pumped into him from one to six inches away.

Two eyewitness versions of the muzzle-distance were brought up by the prosecution. Karl Uecker, who was closest to the victim, said, "two feet." Valerie Schulte, who was the farthest from Sirhan's gun, said it was "three yards" from Bobby.

Ted Charach, a TV producer, who had picked up a film for his documentary, *The Second Gun,* noticed Evelle Younger making the following declaration: "Well, uh... a discrepancy ... if somebody says one inch and somebody else says two inches, that's a discrepancy, but the jury didn't think it was significant and neither did I. What worries me more than a discrepancy in a criminal trial is where you've got all of the witnesses saying exactly the same thing. That's when you have to worry, when there's a reasonable discrepancy."

Charach had asked Noguchi whether it "would be possible to get powder burns if the gun was two or three feet away...?"

"In this case of course, with the abundance of powder

burn imbedded deep in the tissue, it is scientifically unlikely."

One of the experts posed an interesting question. The victim was being escorted eastbound through the hotel kitchen pantry when the murderer, gun in his hand, ran towards him. He fired. Bobby and five other men and women were hit. Among the first to fall was Paul Schrade.

Bobby, as we know, was shot two times in the back at steep upward angles, and once behind the right ear— all at point-blank range. And according to Dr. Noguchi, the head wound was the fatal one.

There were no witnesses that testified seeing the killer closer than one-and-a-half to three feet in front of the victim. And there was no one who testified that Bobby had his back turned to Sirhan at any time.

"Assume," said Harper, "that Sirhan had managed to escape from the scene with the gun, without being seen, what effect would these circumstances have had on the investigation?

"Would the police have been searching for one or two killers?"

The queries were of special concern to many who still refuse to accept the Los Angeles Police Department's version. Schrade and the others wounded expressed doubts about the conclusions drawn by the police, and called for a reinvestigation which got the support of Dr. Robert Jolins, President of the American Academy of Forensic Sciences.

Allard K. Lowenstein was intrigued by the other four bullet holes discovered in the room. Could they have come from Sirhan's eight-shot revolver? What happened to the extra bullets? Later, he learned that the police had removed the panels containing the bullets from the pantry ceiling and destroyed them.

District Attorney Joseph P. Busch Jr. was completely satisfied and said that all the bullets had been accounted for in the official Trajectory Study report prepared by the Crime Lab Chief, DeWayne Wolfer, in 1968, but not released until two years later.

Harper, however, charged that the report was basically an inventory of eight bullets supposedly fired from Sirhan's gun: "It suffered from a dearth of technical details: no measurements of distances or angles were given, nor the locations of the bullet holes and ricochet marks." And while the bullets were numbered, "giving the impression that the time sequence of the various shots was determined," Harper recalled that Noguchi gave autopsy testimony that such a sequence was not determinable, not even the most observant eyewitness tried to say which shot came when."

Uecker was between Bobby and Sirhan when the firing erupted. He and others recalled that Bobby had turned to the left briefly to shake hands with Juan Romero, a busboy, just before Sirhan started to fire. There was no precise agreement whether Bobby turned partially or fully back to face Sirhan.

None testified seeing Sirhan's gun within point-blank range, but the relative positions of Sirhan and Bobby remained a serious issue because the angles of the "wound tracks" in his head and body.

Was Sirhan able to inflict the wounds from any distance because he was firing right-handed from a point just east of the victim? If Kennedy was facing left, the head wound would have been possible. But it would most likely have to emanate from the gun, since he was firing with his right hand.

Eyewitnesses were all certain of one fact: Sirhan was firing with his right hand just over the steam table and around the large form of the overweight Uecker, who blocked his path to the victim.

There was one theory that could perhaps explain the back wounds. It may have been possible for the Jordanian to have shot Kennedy behind the right ear from their relative positions. It would have made Bobby go into a body-spinning position, thus exposing his back to two more bullets from the killer's gun. But none of the witnesses said that they had seen the victim spin around.

Wolfer thought of another possibility. The bullet that penetrated Bobby's right shoulder pad had struck Schrade in the forehead. But Schrade was almost directly behind Bobby's right shoulder— the back-to-front trajectory would have required the victim to have been spun completely around. No eyewitness says that, however. Bobby had been fully turned to the left to shake hands with Juan Romero, so the shoulder-pad bullet could have gone back-to-front.

"But the difficulty that created is that the bullet would then have gone into the North kitchen wall," Lowenstein said, because Bobby was turned in that direction to shake hands with the busboy."

The other possibility was that Kennedy was facing Sirhan and the bullet traveled front-to-back through Bobby's shoulder pad. Lowenstein said that he had discussed that possibility with the Los Angeles Police and with the District

Attorney, who accepted his premise. Lowenstein added: "What troubled me then was how did that bullet go front-to-back while the other bullets that hit Bob Kennedy went back-to-front. You've reduced the number of bullets back to eight because the bullet through the shoulder-pad could have hit Schrade in the head. But haven't you increased the number of guns?"

Another eyewitness, Richard G. Lubic, a TV producer, contended that he didn't believe Sirhan killed Kennedy. When the shooting begun, Lubic dropped to the floor: "As I was on the floor, looking to my left and in back of me, I saw another gun. The gun was pointed in a downward position and it was held by a man in an Ace Guard uniform. I didn't see him shoot."

Daniel L. Schulman, a member of the TV crew, said that he saw the same uniformed security guard from the Ace Guard Service in Van Nuys, California firing his revolver during the commotion in the pantry. But he had decided that he was imagining things. The guard was identified as Eugene Cesar and he worked part-time for the Ace Company. He had been hired to assist in keeping the crowd under control. Cesar admitted pulling his gun in the confusion— a .38 caliber revolver; later he denied it. Again later, he supposedly admitted selling a .22 caliber gun— the same type revolver used by Sirhan— either four or three months before the murder.

After Cesar was interrogated by the local police in 1972, it is said he disappeared. In any event, a number of people believed that Cesar was the man who had fired the second gun. Of course, as he was in uniform, he would not have been noticed as much as he might have been.

Although the mysterious Cesar was living in Los Angeles, not one law enforcement person made any attempt to contact him.

In an interview with reporters of *Der Stern,* Uecker said that "The revolver was directly in front of my nose... I have always said that the shots could not have been fired by Sirhan."

Lubic agreed: "That gun was about this far [two feet] from Bobby's head, not one inch. To this day I don't believe Sirhan killed him."

When Busch was questioned about those contentions, he said, "the inability of people to relate what they see is a frailty of human nature." The day after, he made another statement: "The basic fact remains that a number of eyewitnesses saw Sirhan shoot Robert F. Kennedy and did not see anyone else fire a gun in the pantry.

"Scientific tests verified the fact that Sirhan's gun fired the bullets which killed Senator Kennedy."

But the forensic medical people continued to question the so-called scientific tests quoted by Busch. Harper had his doubts about the official conclusions. Lowell W. Bradford (a former director of the Santa Clara County Laboratory of Criminalistics in San Jose, and later a consultant to various government agencies, who had examined photographs of Kennedy and the Weisel bullets— both Harper's taken in 1970, and another Palliscan photogragh study made in 1974), agreed that Wolfer's bullet was called for.

"There was an identification of the perpetrator by witnesses who saw the shooting, but the real link between the Kennedy bullet and Sirhan was Wolfer's testimony about the bullet comparison. Now, if you don't find any matching striations what it means is that Wolfer was wrong. It means that what there is now a disconnection in the problem of proof—that there is no proof to identify Sirhan's gun with the bullet in Kennedy."

Busch and other police experts said that "air oxidation" and "excessive unauthorized handling" over the years "changes" a bullet's special characteristics.

Bradford countered Busch: "I don't believe that from seeing the Balliscan photos. [The bullets] showed beautiful marks with no apparent change." In other words, the marks did not match, he declared. "What you've got in the Sirhan case is unsupported evidence followed by no cross-examination. And now the value of the connelure work that's been done and the rifling-angle work is something to show there's a reasonable cause to go into the question of whether the bullet comparison is accurate. If it isn't then, all of this other stuff has less meaning."

Four of the wounded victims have requested another re-examination of the evidence. A number of highly-regarded forensic medical experts and criminologists questioned the findings, and stated categorically that the case should re-open. The prosecution, for reasons not necessarily motivated to search for the truth, discounted remarks of other experts, and scoffed at the well-meaning Allard Lowenstein, who was accused of being an amateur seeking popularity.

Senator Edward Kennedy, speaking for the family, said that he had decided to accept the official report. Several days before, he had also accepted the findings of the Warren Commission regarding the murder of his brother *Jack.*

The late Lowenstein said that Edward Kennedy "wouldn't talk about Dallas to anyone nor would he let anyone around him talk about it either."

The subject may have been too painful. As a result, he may have opted to let sleeping dogs lie. He saw no reason to continue to sensationalize the tragedies that had befallen his family.

There may be other questions concerning Bobby's murder. A more important one should be: Must we continue to allow those who accept the mandate to represent this American nation to be so ruthlessly gunned down?

Chapter 31
Epilogue

Bobby Kennedy toured the entire nation and spoke to count-less numbers of Mexican Americans, Indians and blacks and to every other citizen of every color and creed. He had expressed a passionate concern for their problems.

Later, much later, McLuhan, a Canadian author, wrote: "Now that Bob Kennedy has left the scene it is easier to see how much bigger he was then the mere candidate role he undertook to perform. His many hidden dimensions appeared less on the rostrum than his spontaneous excursions into the ghettos and in his easy rapport with the surging generosity of young hearts. He strove to do good by stealth. It was his reluctant hero quality that gave integrity and power to his television image."

No one tried to deny that he was a pugnacious man. As the next to the youngest of the Kennedy males and the smallest in size, he had had to develop such traits to make himself be seen and heard. It led him into a number of excesses at times, and those traits made many people believe he was ruthless.

Jim Bishop, the writer-reporter, did not like him and made that clear in many of his books. Gore Vidal once had an argu-ment with him at the White House and became one of his most persistent critics, a professional Bobby hater. He wrote that his former friend was just "a conventional politician [who was] cautious to the point of timidity. At the same time he was emotionally committed to rhetoric if not the substance of reform. He also expressed doubt if he had the means intellectu-ally or morally to cope with the new necessities."

One young Reform Democrat did not like him when she first met him in 1960. She said that "One should not judge the character of a man by hearing him talk for a half hour at a meeting of politicians." After expressing those thoughts, she added that "he was a passionate man and he involved himself emotionally in a cause," that he didn't give a damn about any-thing except his own immediate objectives, that he seemed to need sycophancy, that he played ball with every cruddy politician in New York to reach his ends, and that basically Bobby just "was not a good guy."

There was more to Bobby than was apparent to Miss Kovner. He was indeed a passionate man, and emotionally involved in a cause, that of the underprivileged. During his early years, he tried to cleanse the unions of their corrupt leaders— a truly Herculean task. He was able to send Teamster Union President Beck to jail. And after many years, he was finally able to get Hoffa convicted.

His methods did leave him wide open for valid criticism. Professor Bickel, the eminent legal mind, wrote many articles deploring the use of the wiretap and the use of the Fifth Amendment. At the same time, Bickel admitted no one could deny that Bobby had been outraged on seeing how the poor and the helpless were being treated in affluent America.

While traveling in the West, he visited Indian reservations where he saw their sufferings. When an aide said he was wasting his time because Indians do not vote, Bobby retorted: "You don't care about suffering."

Lowenstein, who knew Bobby well and who was to become one of his fervent admirers, said that Bobby "was one who seemed to symbolize the conscience of the country."

And Pete Hamill said that "the closer you got to him, the better we liked him."

In California, Bobby had seen first-hand how the migrant workers were being exploited and said that it was "indecent to have men work in the fields and have their sons go off to war."

He was very patient with young people, especially those disowning the values of their elders: "They have struggled and sacrificed alone too long. This is a war surrounded by rhetoric they do not understand or accept. These are the children not of the Cold War, but of the thaw. Their memories are not about Stalin's purges and death camps, not even the terrible revelations of the 20th [Communist] Party Congress or the streets of Hungary."

He looked at corruption and the bloodbaths taking place all over the world and found them to be a stench in his nostrils.

Bobby Kennedy was a strange mixture of shyness and distrust. Not by any means humble, he was prone to impatience and impulsiveness, but he was always a loyal friend and completely devoid of guile.

He was no concocter of political theories, nor was he dogmatic. Deeply religious, during the last moments of his life he held a rosary in his hands. His mother, Rose Kennedy, said that Bobby "had always taken his religion seriously... As a young boy, he served as an altar boy. He never expressed any doubts about his religion. His father once said, 'I always felt that if I died Bob would be the one to keep the family together.' Bob is a disciple of my theory. If you have a family with you, you have a head start on others who must rely on making friends."

He was fiercely loyal to his family and to his many friends. In exchange, Adam Walinsky, Peter Edelstein, Young Turks, Pete Ha mill, Allard Lowenstein, Ken O'Donnel and many many others gave him their complete loyalty. They considered him the "strongest advocate of humanism in America."

Schlesinger once wrote that Bobby "had inherited a tradition as a Democrat of this country, the Democratic Party had been the popular party in America, the party of human rights and social justice." Schlesinger quoted John F. Kennedy as having remarked that Bobby "might once have been intolerant of liberals as such, because his early experience was with the high-minded kind who never get anything done. That all changed the moment he met a liberal like Walter Reuther."

As the Attorney General, Bobby was not the usual kind of prosecutor. He established an Office of Criminal Justice which served as a vehicle to assist the poor in the nation's courts. He also served as Chairman of the President's Committee on Juvenile Delinquency, bringing a number of programs into being. He also helped set up Vista. Rather than a prosecutor, he once said that the Attorney General must see to it that justice is "evenly distributed to both the poor and the wealthy."

Robert Francis Kennedy had traveled a great distance morally from the time he had served as Counsel to the McCarthy Committee. He had become a *Tribune* for the people. As a result, he had dreams of a better America and was not content to have his ideals languish. At a time when he was to ease the plight of his fellow-citizens, and to steer the ship of state into a safe harbor of peace and goodwill, he was struck down by an assassin's bullet.

The mantle dropped from the inert fingers of the slain leader. His younger brother, Ted, aspires to wage the good battle for the poor and for the forgotten. In this time of counter-revolution, there is no one to champion the programs instituted by Franklin Delano Roosevelt and by other advocates of social justice.

At a mass in Bobby's memory at St. Patrick's Cathedral in New York City, Ted Kennedy read the same lines that his brother quoted time and again from George Bernard Shaw:

"Some men see things as they are and say, *Why?* I read things that never were and say, *Why not!*"

BOBBY, TED, AND JOHN POSING AT THE WHITE HOUSE

THE LAST FAMILY PICTURE